At a time when many parents and ed_____ where the world is heading and abo_____ this world, Tony Ryan offers a positi_____ we can't refuse. In this book, he paints an astonishing range of possibilities and pictures of what's up ahead and offers practical guidance on essential capabilities our next generation will need to thrive and lead productive, fulfilling lives. A must read for anyone who cares about preparing young people well to make the most of their extraordinary futures.

Joan Dalton, Education Advisor

Hope is at the heart of the human condition. Tony Ryan's brilliant and at times provocative exploration of the world that the next generation will inhabit is refreshing and positive. We have a responsibility to ensure that our children have an excitement about the future and the world in which they will engage. Tony's work invites all of us to explore and contribute to our children's future.

Dr Stephen Brown, internationally renowned educator and expert on school leadership

Tony Ryan's work has a specific quality. Attention. He sees possibility. Combining enthusiastic wonder with rigorous enquiry, this futurist mounts a case that today's young people can look ahead to the mid 21st century with optimism.

Bill Jennings, Founder of Time & Space (Parent-Child Programs)

Tony is a futurist focused on inspiring change and creating positive impact. He has a deep passion for young people and helping them thrive in the future. Tony explores the edge of possibility then makes sense of this so that we can then help our young people be extraordinary. This is a book of optimism, hope and social action.

Dr Cheryl Doig, Leadership Futurist

Tony Ryan is one of the most exciting educators I know. I especially love talking with him about the future of education and the world. He really blows my mind with the stuff he talks about and I can't help wondering if he has actually been to the future and come back!

Professor Chris Sarra, University of Canberra, Chairman, Stronger Smarter Institute

Tony Ryan's brilliance shines through once again. He gives teachers, students and parents hope for a bright future with practical and commonsense offerings. This is a must read for everyone with a vested interest in the success of our youth.

Karen Boyes, CEO Spectrum Education, Speaker, Author, Parent

Anxiety affects one in FIVE children worldwide. It's no wonder. We continually subject them to messages that have little hope for the future. It's time to turn this around. Children really can learn resilience and positive coping skills that will help them develop an optimistic thinking style about the world together with increased 'thumbs up' choices. This inspiring book will contribute to those choices. If anyone is going to convince our children that the future just might be extraordinary, it is Tony Ryan. His message is balanced, consistent and has every chance of becoming a reality.

Dr Paula Barrett, Author of the Friends Resilience Programs
www.FriendsResilience.org

The educator's Educator, Tony Ryan is a thinker with purpose and passion for the community. Never in history have there been so many incredible opportunities on offer for our youth, yet there is a ubiquitous negativity in the mainstream with messages to the contrary — these messages are informing and forming our youngest minds. Tony's book provides a much needed counterpoint for parents, teachers and education authorities at a time when lifting the narrative around optimism and opportunity has never been more important.

Sean Gordon, Founder and Executive Director, SchoolAid Trust, Life Member of the Australian Primary Principals Association

Leading educator and futurist, Tony Ryan, has one of the sharpest minds on the planet. His excitement and optimism about the future are contagious and a sharp contrast to the pessimism pushed in the media. This is essential reading for all parents and educators.

Steve Francis, Education Expert

Today's adolescents are educated to believe that the futuristic society will be flawed. Having this mindset has discouraged the genuine reality that the future is open to limitless, phenomenal possibilities. If only students were optimistic enough to see the world as the bright place it will be. This book will help everyone to think about those possibilities.

Fran Turner, age 13

Tony Ryan is a passionate educator who cares deeply about making the world a better place through harnessing the amazing capacity of our young people. Through his work he provides educators with a window into our future world and the limitless possibilities. His optimism and enthusiasm is contagious as he challenges our thinking and shares insights about how we can engage more effectively with the learners in our care. A vibrant speaker, insightful author and engaging teacher, Tony has been a positive influence on the lives of so many people across the globe. He is truly inspirational.

Faye Hauwai, CEO Learning Network NZ

THE NEXT GENERATION

THE NEXT GENERATION

PREPARING TODAY'S KIDS
FOR AN EXTRAORDINARY FUTURE

TONY RYAN

WILEY

First published in 2018 by John Wiley & Sons Australia, Ltd
42 McDougall St, Milton Qld 4064
Office also in Melbourne

Typeset in 12.5/14.5 pt Bembo Std

© Headfirst Publishing Pty Ltd 2018

The moral rights of the author have been asserted

National Library of Australia Cataloguing-in-Publication data:

Creator:	Ryan, Tony J., author.
Title:	The next generation: preparing today's kids for an extraordinary future / Tony Ryan.
ISBN:	9780730345046 (pbk.)
	9780730345053 (ebook)
Notes:	Includes index.
Subjects:	Future, The,
	Social prediction
	Economic forecasting.
	Technology and youth — 21st century
	Education — 21st century.
	Life skills–Study and teaching.

Cover design Kathy Davis/Wiley

Cover image © Teenagers with gadgets: GeorgeRudy/iStockphoto;
Black and White Printed Circuit Board: mastaka/iStockphoto

Printed in Singapore by C.O.S. Printers Pte Ltd

10 9 8 7 6 5 4 3 2 1

Disclaimer
The material in this publication is of the nature of general comment only, and does not represent professional advice. It is not intended to provide specific guidance for particular circumstances and it should not be relied on as the basis for any decision to take action or not take action on any matter which it covers. Readers should obtain professional advice where appropriate, before making any such decision. To the maximum extent permitted by law, the author and publisher disclaim all responsibility and liability to any person, arising directly or indirectly from any person taking or not taking action based on the information in this publication.

To Sharon

CONTENTS

ABOUT THE AUTHOR

Tony Ryan is an education futurist. A parent and a teacher himself, he helps educators and parents throughout the world to understand and prepare for the future of schooling and the workplace.

In the past two decades, he has directly worked with over 1000 schools, colleges, TAFEs and universities in Australia, the United States, New Zealand, Singapore, Malaysia, Hong Kong, China, Indonesia, Canada, and Mexico.

He is the author of *The Ripple Effect, Thinkers Keys, Mindlinks, Wrapped In Living* and a series of manuals and workbooks that stimulate innovative thinking in children.

Tony is a former national president of Professional Speakers Australia, a former board chairman of School Aid Trust, and is presently an Australian ambassador for their cause. He is the co-founder of School2School, an organisation that encourages first world schools to support schools in less developed countries.

ACKNOWLEDGEMENTS

Imagine being able to engage and learn with 1000s of inspiring people every year. This is the blessing of my life. I work with parents and educators all over the world who are raising our Next Generation with care, determination and unswerving belief in their contribution. I will be forever grateful that they have allowed me to engage with them.

It might take a village to raise a child, but it takes a tribe to support the writing of a book about those children and their future. The first and foremost member of that tribe is my wife and lifelong partner Sharon, who has a beautiful mind and soul; and was the best ever sounding board when it was needed during the writing. Naomi is the most awesome daughter anyone could have; and I'm lucky enough that she's mine. Her creative genius enlivens all discussion about the future. My grand-daughter Dana is a gift in my life, and already demonstrates what the Next Generation will accomplish.

Joan Dalton is the most outstanding educator in the world (and that's saying something!). Without her editorial advice in the initial stages of writing, this book would not have happened. She resonates with its core intent as strongly as I do, and I'll be forever grateful for her support.

My perceptive niece Kate Davies offered some superb suggestions for the chapter on 'All in a day's work'. Thanks also to the rest of my gorgeous family — my mother Maureen, who is my greatest fan;

my supremely talented sisters Tricia and Mary-louise; Patrick, Terry, Glenn, Matthew, Linda, Owen, and especially Hugh.

So many other high achievers believed in the book's message, and gave support accordingly. The intuitive Alie Blackwell can scan an early draft for just a few minutes, and then offer the most incisive and compelling advice. Sporting mate Dr Timo Dietrich provided invaluable support with digital marketing and web development.

A very special group of talented people offered an endorsement. They are each a tribute to education and parenting. Endless thanks to Michael Grose, Joan Dalton, Bill Jennings, Dr Stephen Brown, Dr Cheryl Doig, Professor Chris Sarra, Karen Boyes, Dr Paula Barrett, Sean Gordon, Steve Francis, Fran Turner, and Faye Hauwai.

The Wiley crew has been hugely supportive. This book is so many degrees better than it would have been without them. Lucy Raymond was my initial contact, and totally has her heart in publishing. Jem Bates thankfully tempered my exuberant enthusiasm with his insightful and measured editing. Talented editor Chris Shorten shadowed me every step of the way, and has made the process more seamless and enjoyable for me. Theo Vassili was always supportive of my provocative conjectures on marketing. May they all continue to superbly support the literary world.

INTRODUCTION
A CALL TO ACTION

What are we doing to our young people? This is the best time in human history to be alive, and the future offers such amazing potential. Yet we constantly overwhelm them with how difficult the world up ahead might be.

While the future might be a complex and unpredictable place, that doesn't mean we can't positively influence what will occur. On the contrary, we have more control over that future than we might initially think.

In many ways, we can even create what is up ahead; and we need to help our kids to believe that they can do this too. One recent experience brought home to me the importance of encouraging this hope and creative capacity for the future in our young people.

For the past seven years, I have presented an annual Rotary talk to 100 young leaders from all walks of life. My session is on social contribution and how exciting the world up ahead can be.

At the conclusion of my latest presentation, I was approached by several of the attendees. They said it was heartening to hear such optimistic messages, and that they rarely heard such upbeat views from anyone.

According to them, every single adult in their lives, including their parents and their community leaders, consistently griped about the state of the world and maintained there was little chance of the future being any better. In fact, their elders often insisted it would be much worse.

It's time to turn this around. Let's dump the scare campaigns that leave our Next Generation feeling helpless, and instead show them how their choices today can create an inspiring future.

Rather than asking them, 'What's the world going to be like up ahead?', ask, 'What sort of world do you *want* to create up ahead?' The first question suggests they have no control over it, while the second demonstrates they do.

If you want to help children engage with the second question, this book is for you. It is organised in three sections:

◊ **Part I. What's up ahead for our children.** These introductory chapters clarify some of the exciting possibilities with our children's future, with a focus on the mind-altering world of technology and the manner in which it will influence work choices.

◊ **Part II. Essential capabilities.** Facing an uncertain future, today's children will require the critical capabilities outlined in these three chapters — specifically, adaptive agility, empathy and a love of inquiry.

◊ **Part III. Actions for creating an extraordinary life.** These concluding chapters offer three approaches to putting the knowledge in this book into everyday practice — through enterprise, philanthropy, and action projects.

The best time to plant a tree, according to the Chinese proverb, was 20 years ago. The second-best time is now. Let's get started.

PART I

WHAT'S UP AHEAD FOR OUR CHILDREN

CHAPTER 1

A window into possibility: coping with the beautiful mess

WHAT IT'S ABOUT

Today's children will become tomorrow's adults in a time of dramatic, often exponential changes. This chapter will explore some of these possible changes, and how we can prepare our children's thinking for the exciting new world they will find. Let's begin by meeting someone who is already creating this amazing future.

#thenextgeneration #promisingfuture #beautifulmess #predictingtheirfuture #transhumanism

A FUTURE FULL OF PROMISE

The future is meant to be a promise, not a threat. If Boyan Slat is any indication, our Next Generation will rise to that promise. This young Dutch entrepreneur is part of the new cohort determined to create an inspiring world up ahead. While he was still a teenager, Slat launched the Ocean Cleanup project,[1] which has been dubbed the largest clean-up in history. His astounding proposal? That up to 40 per cent of all rubbish in the world's oceans be removed within 10 years.

This is no small ambition. About eight million tonnes of plastic enters our oceans every year, and the cost of conventional removal methods is prohibitive. Slat asked, Why move through the ocean with a clean-up, when the ocean can move through you? His ingenious system relies on the ocean's currents collecting the debris inside what is called an Ocean Cleanup Array. Much of the oceans' rubbish presently accumulates in five ocean garbage patches around the world. In 2017, the first pilot installation of an array became operational in the largest of them all—the Great Pacific Garbage Patch between Hawaii and California.

> Their unprecedented entrepreneurial involvement will unleash one of the greatest economic and social evolutions in human history.

Boyan Slat is just one of millions of energetic young entrepreneurs determined to make the world an even better place. Around thirty-five per cent of the world's population is under 20 years old.[2] It is they who will become the movers and shakers of the 21st century. Many already are. With increased access to the internet, and to learning opportunities that were simply not available at the start of the century, this generation will transform the planet. Nearly 90 per cent of these under-20s live in emerging countries in Africa, the Middle East, South America and Asia.[3] Their unprecedented entrepreneurial involvement will unleash one of the greatest economic and social evolutions in human history.

For the purposes of this book, the Next Generation refers to two cohorts: Gen Z (born between 1994 and 2009); and Gen Alpha (born after 2009). These young people, who will become the leaders of the mid 21st century, will be the most educated in human history.[4] Approaching the 22nd century, they will experience techno-enhanced lifestyles far beyond our present imagination.[5]

This is a good time for them to be alive. Most people in the future are likely to live much longer than those who came before them. Since 1900, average life expectancy has more than doubled.[6] First-year infant mortality has dropped from 19.5 per cent to 3.69 per cent.[7] Global poverty has plummeted from 44 per cent to around 10 per cent in the past 30 years.[8]

Here is one improvement in this new millennium that will astound most adults. Our present Gen Zs behave better than their parents did at their age.[9, 10] You may want to think carefully before you share this information with your resident teenager. Rates of a wide range of discouraged behaviours such as smoking, drinking and even (gasp) sexual activity are much lower than for the previous generation.

Does this mean they are behaving perfectly? Of course not. There are still problems. Today's children are more overweight, and some of their dietary habits need lots of attention. Teenage depression appears to be on the rise. Sporadic violence by a small number is unsettling. A minority become cyber-addicted, and a few engage in cyber-bullying. However, the overall landscape can be viewed with some degree of optimism.

For the sake of our children and their future, let's set the record straight. Most indicators (although not all) clearly show that the standard of living has improved dramatically for many people around the world. Right now there are countless projects taking place that are as inspiring as the Ocean Cleanup, and they have been developed by young people who want to make life better for all of us.

But let's pause for a moment and consider: is everything really all that wonderful?

THE WORLD IS A BEAUTIFUL MESS

It's two and a half minutes to midnight right now, according to the Doomsday Clock, featured in the *Bulletin of the Atomic Scientists*.[11] First introduced in 1947, this symbolic clock face represents the assessment of a group of eminent scientists as to how close the world is hypothetically to nuclear disaster. In 2007, its brief was expanded to include the danger of catastrophic climate change. Its time setting has varied over the years, from a relatively optimistic 17 minutes to midnight in 1991 to the present more pessimistic evaluation.

If you are a pessimist looking for evidence that the world is in trouble, you will find plenty to justify your personal belief. Terrorist threats, global warming, refugee resettlement, youth underemployment, worldwide economic debt, and the increasing divide between rich and poor are probably never far from your mind ... and they're only the long-term concerns.

We are also vulnerable to a litany of one-off events with the potential to reshape world history. Natural disasters, solar flares, recalcitrant robots, cyberwars and perhaps even the occasional meteorite could compromise all life on planet Earth. Will there be more of these types of events? You can bet your life on it.

So we can hardly say that life is perfect right now. Then what about the future? Will our children's world be entirely optimistic? Probably not. Will it be deeply pessimistic? That's equally improbable. The world of the future will most likely be a beautiful mess. It has always been so, and it always will be. So whose predictions are more valid, the optimists' or the pessimists'? Given that optimists invented the aeroplane and pessimists invented the parachute, both perspectives are useful.

There is another, more attractive perspective, though. *Realistic optimism* means a healthy balance between the two opposites. Think of people who keep an open mind to all possibilities while still applying a healthy degree of

> The world of the future will most likely be a beautiful mess. It has always been so, and it always will be.

scepticism in their thinking. The future needs lots of these realistic optimists more than it does those at either end of the spectrum. Over-trusting optimists and bitter pessimists are less likely to live a satisfying life. Here's why.

When you trust everyone and everything as an arch-optimist, you can fall prey to those who take advantage of your unquestioning nature. Even when the evidence indicates there is a problem, you will still convince yourself it's not true. You want to believe the world is perfect. If you are too pessimistic, on the other hand, you will miss out on many opportunities, convinced that there is a trap in there somewhere. You probably worry much more than is necessary, to the detriment of your own welfare.

Pessimists did indeed invent the parachute, but they also risk becoming entangled in its cords. Standing in the same prison cell, some people see bars where others see stars. French writer Anaïs Nin once wrote, 'We don't see the world as it is. We see it as we are'. When someone sees the worst in everything, this may not be a reflection of the world around them. It is just as likely to be a reflection of their inner world.

Imagine if pessimists were to reprogram their amygdalae. These two almond-shaped sets of neurons in our brain react to circumstances that are dangerous, rather than to ones that are safe and positive. In our distant past, this kept us cautious and alive. For most of us, today's risks are less dramatic. The dilemma is that our amygdalae fuel a negativity bias that compels us to pay more attention to what is going badly than to what is going well. And this bias is reinforced by most news bulletins in the mass media.

> The better things get, the worse we think they are.

The negativity bias has led to a perverse belief: the better things get, the worse we think they are. Gregg Easterbrook wrote about this dilemma in *The Progress Paradox*,[12] in which he documented two competing influences. One is the unrelenting improvement in many worldwide indicators of life quality; the second is our steadily diminishing level of happiness and perceived wellbeing over the past 50 years. Too many of us are choosing—or have been convinced—to believe that the world is not a good place, and are less happy as a result. So why is that?

Consider what shapes our thinking every day. Over 90 per cent of news coverage is basically bad news. Are all media journalists negative people? On the contrary, most care deeply about their profession, and pride themselves on providing a reasoned viewpoint. As much as anyone else, the general public are to blame. While we claim to recoil from the more horrendous messages, we signal that we prefer them to the good news. The click-through on negative headlines is 63 per cent higher than on positive headlines.[13] This encourages news broadcasters to deliver more of what people are clicking, given that higher audience numbers improve their advertising potential.

This gives an unbalanced perspective on global news. The vast majority of events in daily life fall somewhere between uneventful and inspiring. Unfortunately, we are fed a burst of choreographed negative news reports, accompanied by suitably sombre or dramatic music, that represent a minute proportion of that everyday life. Is it any wonder that people believe the world is in big trouble? Constant worry about these events consumes their thinking.

Worrying is wasteful. It creates negative energy, tires us out and rather than resolving an issue, can sometimes make it worse. While we know that worry accomplishes little, stopping doing it is another matter. So here's one question to ask yourself and your children: How many of the things you worry about end up happening?

One in ten? Two in ten? If you made the effort to keep a count for the day, you might be surprised by the very low figure. Back in the 16th century, Michel de Montaigne captured this truth when he said, 'My life has been filled with terrible misfortune, most of which never happened'.

If we went back 30 years, we would find that the global worries then current rarely became the catastrophes we expected. We simply applied our human ingenuity and resourcefulness, and whenever possible we created solutions. When today's children look back three decades from now, will they also find that few of our gravest fears eventuated? It's very likely. If only we had the power to predict the future. Is that possible?

CAN WE PREDICT OUR CHILDREN'S FUTURE?

The short answer is no. Anything that is pure chance cannot be predicted. That includes next Saturday night's Lotto-winning numbers, unfortunately. It also applies to most natural disasters. We cannot predict complex social or political developments more than a year away—or often even those much closer to the present—with any degree of accuracy. Such forecasting is nothing more than calculated guesswork. Think of share market movements or decisions made by the North Korean leader as falling into this category.

Here is a guarded 'perhaps' to speculating on anything up ahead. The analysis of everyday data offers some indication of what may occur down the track. We can determine with 70 per cent confidence what children will be doing on this day in exactly two years from now, especially if they are creatures of habit. With predictive policing, we can calculate with up to 90 per cent certainty the likelihood of some teenagers committing an offence.

TALKING WITH
THE NEXT GENERATION

WHEN THEY SAY

'The world is going to be awful up ahead.'

SOME RESPONSES YOU MIGHT OFFER

'It's possible, but it's not very likely. **People have been saying for hundreds of years that the world is going to be awful up ahead, but it all still keeps going.** You need to watch out for the doomsayers who try to scare you about everything in the future. They are nearly always wrong.'

'The world keeps getting better, not worse. While there are certainly lots of big problems we need to resolve, there are many other things that continue to improve. Here's one example: Most people are healthier than they've ever been before, and by the time you're grown up, we will have cures for most illnesses.'

'Admittedly, we can't easily predict the future. It might end up being fantastic, or it might sometimes be problematic. But here's a really important point: **The future is not just something that happens to us. It's something we create.** So start thinking about the sort of future you'd like for yourself and for others up ahead, and then begin to make it happen.'

Medical analysts can assess with 80 per cent confidence whether children will contract the flu, eight days before they actually get it.[14] The GPS on the child's mobile phone can signal where they were today and who was in their group. If anyone in that group indicated on social media they were feeling sick at the time, the child's chances of contracting that illness are much higher, given their proximity to the ill person. However, none of this is outright prediction. It uses data analysis to determine the chances of an event occurring.

Some global events can be calculated very accurately. For example, we know there will be a major solar eclipse on 20 May 2050.[15] Isaac Newton once said, 'I can calculate the movement of the stars but not the madness of men'. He was no doubt swayed by the fact that he had just lost a lot of money in one of the world's first stock-market bubbles.[16]

Sharemarkets tend to follow seven-year cycles, and sunspot activity has an 11-year cycle, although betting your money on exact timing in either case is pretty risky. A group of very smart people called super-forecasters[17] specialise in reading all relevant data and calculating the chances of an event occurring. This may involve no more than determining what will be the most popular Christmas toy a year away. It's still not guaranteed prediction, however. It's about developing a percentage probability.

> Our best course is to prepare ourselves for whatever might occur up ahead.

Our best course is to prepare ourselves for whatever might occur up ahead. We stay fit and healthy to stave off illness in the future. Some people save money for a rainy day. We make the effort to raise beautiful kids so they can live a fulfilling adulthood. Great parents and educators build up capabilities in children so they will thrive, whatever happens in the years ahead. One of the great secrets to doing this is to implement protective factors. These are interventions in children's lives that lead to healthy development, and might involve mentoring, friendships, and engagement in sport and recreational activities.

On the opposite side, risk factors are negative effects that compromise child development. They include events that cause anxiety and toxic stress. The world will be an even better place in 20 years' time if we minimise the risk factors and maximise the protective factors in kids' lives today. A targeted intervention is always warranted for a risk factor such as anxiety. Many great platforms, such as the Australian-based FRIENDS program,[18] have validated the positive changes that take place in children when they practise anxiety-reducing skills.

Mentoring programs are a powerful example of a protective factor. Children need supportive role models who show them what it means to be an inspiring and responsible adult. A Toronto study in 2013 determined that $1 invested in mentoring programs leads to an eventual $18 return. A child involved in an extensive mentoring program will earn, on average, $315 000 more in a lifetime than another child in a control group that did not receive this support.[19]

In some cultures, parents have the patience and wisdom to think many generations ahead. They understand that every protective factor today contributes to their children becoming more worthy adults later in life. Thinking ahead like this has become more complicated, though.

In the next 20 years, we will experience much more rapid change and increased complexity than in the past 20. Preparing today's children for the future is vastly more complicated and will require an advanced thinking capacity. To do this preparation we won't just need to think outside the square; we will need to explore the boundaries of what is possible.

EXPLORING THE EDGE OF POSSIBILITY

Prepare yourself and your children for a Second Renaissance of extraordinary innovation. This near future may include additive printers and molecular reassemblers that can create most physical products at minimal cost. The sale of products may be displaced by an economy based predominantly on intellectual property. The concept of scarcity could be supplanted by an environmentally sustainable abundance of low-cost goods and services for all people.

Work, in its present form, may become a distant memory, superseded by a hybrid synergy between humans and artificial intelligence. All education and training may be provided by advanced one-on-one personalised artificial intelligence systems. Housing, constructed by giant 3D printers, could be one-tenth of its present cost. Each of these prospects is speculative, although they are all distinct possibilities.

How far might these technologies expand? Most of them will pale into insignificance if teleportation is ever developed. The capacity to travel across the world in an instant would revolutionise the transport industry! Facebook have committed to a form of teleportation by 2025 — on a virtual platform, at least.[20] However, the National Technological Initiative, a Russian consortium that directs massive funding into state-sponsored development, predicts it will have developed basic teleportation by 2035.[21]

Early efforts will involve the transfer of very simple forms of matter, but the eventual realisation of human teleportation would comprehensively alter the way we live on planet Earth. Will we see it in the next 100 years? It's unlikely, although you learn to never say never when it comes to future possibilities. Science fiction has a way of becoming science fact.

Such an exhilarating future may require ways of thinking beyond our present capabilities. In chapter 2, we will explore whether our children will require brain augmentation to match advances in artificial intelligence. But here's a different perspective. There is an all-natural option for improving our thinking. What if we learned how to fully utilise the vast untapped potential of our own brain?

We are already beginning to do so. The 'Flynn effect'[22] proposes that human IQ has been progressing far beyond normal evolutionary limits over the past century. James Flynn claims we are smarter than our grandparents, which could generate some interesting arguments at your next family gathering. His study has revealed a

13.8-point increase in IQ scores around the world between 1932 and 1978, which is approximately three points per decade.

This is a remarkable change in a short period of human history. While some further studies are now indicating that this effect is levelling out, the mental stimulus from exposure to advanced education, let alone endless YouTube videos and Dr Google's advice, is unprecedented. This exposure helps to stimulate and improve our thinking.

Two well-funded projects launched in 2013 have accelerated our understanding of the human brain. The US program, the BRAIN Initiative,[23] will develop ever more complex and revolutionary interpretations of the brain's functions. Europe's Human Brain Project[24] has been exploring contemporary understandings of neuroscience.

Our own brains may have potential far beyond that of any present or future machine. The savant syndrome offers insight into this potential. Autistic savants generally have an IQ between 40 and 70, but they demonstrate one outstanding skill. This prodigious talent can range from memorising all the streets in a suburb to the ability to recite the entire Bible from memory. Are such potential facilities locked up in all of us?

Savant expert Darold Treffert believes they are. He proposes that we are all born with a genetic memory that was 'factory-installed', and it is this that the savants access.[25] Other people cannot retrieve this vast memory, according to Treffert, partly because they have been conditioned along well-worn mental pathways from an early age.

> Tomorrow's remarkable technology may challenge us to become more aware of our own prodigious abilities.

Treffert believes everyone may eventually be able to access this genetic memory. Other scientists disagree, proposing instead that savants receive earlier exposure to the prodigious quantities of material they have mastered. According to these scientists, this instruction is implicit rather than explicit. In either case, the savant talent remains astonishingly impressive.

Nobel laureate James D. Watson once said, 'The brain boggles the mind'.[26] It does indeed. Tomorrow's remarkable technology may challenge us to become even more aware of our own prodigious cognitive capacities. The headwear iPhone 18 may enable us to transmit thought messages to others, but we may eventually discover that we can do this without using the headwear. Welcome to the future possibilities of mental telepathy.

Does this sound too far-fetched? Perhaps it is. However, the challenge with thinking about the world ahead for our children is that we are anchored to our present thinking patterns and understandings. If we were able to go back to visit the 1870s, and tried to explain to people then what was happening today, it would be incomprehensible to them. Imagine describing social media to someone who still uses the telegraph. Consider what might occur if we were visited by time travellers from 2120 who described that future world.

Their version of social media might be a form of global brain or collective consciousness, in which millions co-create intuitively to initiate changes in world affairs. We would struggle to grasp what was being outlined to us, yet for those visitors from the future, personal telepathy and the global brain would be taken for granted.

Transhumanism,[27] meaning 'beyond human', is about the rapid enhancement or transformation of our present human state. Opportunities in this field of study will open up well before 2050. We may need this movement. A convergence of mega-issues will require a depth of thinking and awareness that transcends pre–21st century efforts. How will this be done? The critical first step is to focus on the planet's most vital project.

THE POTENTIAL OF THE FUTURE

The world's most important project is to raise our children with love, guidance and a belief that they can live great lives. Billions of parents, grandparents, carers and education professionals already do this every day. The quality of their teaching will determine the quality of human life in the mid 21st century. It's the sort of 'big picture' concern that gets us all out of bed in the morning.

In the chapters that follow I outline many wonderful improvements that are presently being implemented around the world. The initiative and ingenuity of people everywhere will very likely fill you with awe and gratitude. They certainly generated wonder in me as I researched this book. Just look at what we have accomplished in recent history.

> The quality of their teaching will determine the quality of human life in the mid 21st century.

Five hundred years ago, people would have shaken their heads in disbelief at the notion that the global literacy rate would soar from 5 per cent to 95 per cent; or that the murder rate in the 21st century would be one-thirtieth of what it was back then; or that vast improvements in sanitation and medical science would more than double the human lifespan.

Many recent improvements have been rapid and sustainable. The proportion of income spent on food has halved in the past 50 years. Under-five mortality rates have dropped by 50 per cent in the past 25 years. The number of children involved in hazardous work conditions and performing child labour has been falling since 2000, when it stood at 246 million, and is expected to drop below 107 million by 2020, before eventually decreasing to zero.[28, 29]

There is a realistic possibility that in the next few decades we may eliminate global hunger, provide clean drinking water for everyone and a full education for every child, and eradicate most major diseases that exist today. While technology alone will not solve these problems, the human ingenuity that applies it certainly will.

CHAPTER 2

Hybrid humanity: preparing for the robot–human interface

WHAT IT'S ABOUT

By the mid 21st century, our children's physical and mental capabilities will be greatly enhanced by technology. At the same time, robots will be demonstrating advanced human-like traits. This chapter explores the increasingly blurred distinction between humans and robots, and offers some challenging illustrations. Let's start with Pepper, who is not your average robot.

#emotionalrobots #robotrelationships #advancedbodies
#artificialintelligence #smarterchildren

A DAILY DOSE OF PEPPER THE ROBOT

Pepper[1] is not your everyday domestic robot. Jointly developed in 2014 by robotics companies Aldebaran (Paris) and SoftBank (Tokyo), Pepper robots now welcome customers into retail stores throughout Japan. They live in private Japanese homes, they are receptionists in European hospitals, and they work in American car dealerships, grocery stores and even elementary schools for disabled children.

What's so special about Pepper, given there is nothing new about robot helpers in factories, hospitals and homes? Pepper has been designed to interact with you in an *emotional* way — at least for a robot. By using face and voice recognition technology, it (he?) can identify the expressions on your face, interpret your voice and even engage you in conversation.

Can humans really relate with non-living entities such as Pepper? According to roboticists researching the human–robot interface, most people express a degree of affinity with robots.[2] Humans also respond as though they believe robots do care about them in some basic way.

This response may be triggered by various signals from the robot. Pepper's eyes change colour during a conversation, his tone of voice adjusts to your mood, and his chest panel displays images that reinforce what he says. Want to vent your feelings about a problem? Pepper is there for you. At the time of writing, he costs around US$1800. For maintenance and insurance over the first three years of ownership, add an extra US$8000.

How would you and your family respond to having a Pepper in your own home? Imagine you have just won a promotional competition. The prize is a Pepper robot that will live with you for six months. Your children's enthusiastic response makes you feel as if you have won a national lottery. Your son Charlie programs the new arrival on the day of delivery. Pepper eventually becomes a much-loved addition to the family, and you all wonder how you ever managed without him.

18

So how would your family react if someone deliberately damaged Pepper? If a person purposely trod on your mobile phone, you would probably become a little upset. Would you react more strongly to an attack on Pepper, given his perceived emotional connection with you? If you feel strongly about this right now, then how will your children respond to new generations of empathic robots they will encounter in their adulthood?

Today, a nine-year-old can sit in the corner of a classroom, happily engrossed in reading a book to a small robot, and give this fusion of metal and plastic a hug at the end of the story. As robots further refine their emotional range—albeit artificially simulated—might a child in 30 years' time want to protect her robot from any assault or 'pain'? More than half of the children in a University of Washington study[3] felt it was unfair when a robot was locked away in a cupboard against its expressed wishes.

> More than half of the children in a University of Washington study felt it was unfair when a robot was locked away in a cupboard against its expressed wishes.

Let's consider your family's possible response to Pepper. When the six-month loan is over, you all find that the thought of parting with him is too much to bear. You make a collective decision to purchase him, and with regular maintenance and software upgrades he continues to function as effectively as ever. Eventually, five years from now, the day comes when he needs to be replaced.

What happens to him after he is taken away, you ask. 'We recycle every component,' you are told. 'He is disassembled, the metal is melted down, and a 3D printer robot replicator creates a new Pepper.' Hearing this, you find your lip is quivering and tears begin to well up. You think back to the time when a much-loved pet had to be euthanised, and you decide you just cannot go through that grief again.

OUR CHILDREN'S FUTURE RELATIONSHIPS WITH ROBOTS

That story may sound a little ridiculous, although there are already political moves to safeguard robot rights. In May 2016, a draft motion was presented to the European Commission asking members to consider 'that at least the most sophisticated autonomous robots could be established as having the status of electronic persons with specific rights and obligations'.[4]

Such a motion is unlikely to pass in the European Parliament, given resistance from robot manufacturers and other industrial entities. Their general response is that such a proposal is being considered too soon. Does that mean they will willingly revisit the question when robots become more advanced?

We are entering a dramatic new robot age. The hybridisation of human and artificial entities will challenge our children to rethink all relationships on the planet, including human-to-human, human-to-robot and even robot-to-robot connections.

Robots will become more 'lifelike', acting increasingly like human beings. Today's household robots may look like little more than toys, but they will eventually become highly competent in many fields. What if they become independent of or even inimical to humans? Might advances in humanoid robotics give rise to destructive scenarios? Public luminaries such as Stephen Hawking, Elon Musk and Bill Gates suggest we need to be careful.[5]

Others consider such speculation as little more than scaremongering while pointing out that the benefits of AI applications will far outweigh the risks.[6] It's impossible to predict the nature of the robot–human interface in the 22nd century, although it is plausible that robots will become steadily more integrated into our children's world, immeasurably enhancing the quality of their lives. The part played by emotion in that interaction will be interesting.

At some point on a compassion scale, robots may become more competent than most humans at communicating with people. These robots may serve our children in cafés, drive their cars, fly their planes, do their paperwork and perform brain surgery on them. But will these metallic assistants remain merely servants, or might they become friends or partners? Some believe that sexbots will become increasingly commonplace.

Might humans and robots one day bond and even marry, as some futurists have suggested?[7] While most people today would be aghast at the thought—and after years of pondering this scenario I confess I am too—others may find the prospect appealing. Given the exponential advances in robotics likely in the next 30 years, the non-human partner in the marriage will be in many respects remarkably human-like.

The negative implications of this human–robot interface include the loss of human intimacy and undermining of loving human relationships. Perhaps most intriguing is the idea that a human might actually prefer a robot to other human beings.

And what about the first dinner party where your son Charlie introduces his robot spouse to the family? In times past, a partner of different ethnicity, religion or culture would cause consternation among some groups. Will we see similar scenes regarding robot relationships in the 2040s? How would you respond to such an event with your own children? We can only hope that your open-mindedness and sense of humour would remain intact.

There may be merit in such connections, improbable as they might seem today. Think about the intimate needs of disabled people who have struggled to find a partner. Or consider the lowered incidence of sexually transmitted diseases in the community, assuming that the rate of human liaisons falls. What of loneliness, and the companionship such a bond might offer a socially isolated individual? Perhaps we will soon see dating sites where humans can match themselves with the robot of their dreams.

Hold on, I hear people say. This is just too much. Artificial intelligence surely can never be fully human, and we must resist this threat to human relationships at every opportunity. Perhaps, although throughout human history as we have advanced technologically, new technologies have had both positive and negative consequences. A realistic optimist would not dismiss robotics out of hand, but would carefully assess the possible benefits of each application.

> A realistic optimist would not dismiss robotics out of hand, but would carefully assess the possible benefits of each application.

What sets these developments in robotics apart is that at their core they challenge what it means to be human. Perhaps the intangible concept of 'soul' will become the determinant of our humanity, although futurist Ray Kurzweil talks of the possibility of spiritual machines by the 2040s. Adding to this complexity, future physical enhancements will not be restricted to robots. Because as they become more advanced, so will we.

REFINEMENTS TO THE HUMAN BODY

New York–based avant-garde artist Neil Harbisson has a permanent antenna implanted in his skull.[8] Neil was born with an extreme form of colour blindness. His antenna uses audible vibrations in his skull to signal different information to him. As well as identifying music and electromagnetic radiation, he can 'listen to' light frequencies across the spectrum, which allows him to determine the colour of an object. He can also detect satellite signals, and even receive direct phone calls!

If this sort of embedded technology makes you uncomfortable, you're not alone. A Pew Research Center survey of US adults in July 2016[9] found that more than half of all adults would not want any form of enhancement to their body or brain. Most people said they would be 'very' or 'somewhat' worried about gene editing (68 per cent), brain chips (69 per cent) or synthetic blood (63 per cent). Just as many people said they would not want enhancements to their brain (66 per cent).

The question of gene editing was more evenly split, with 50 per cent reporting they would not want it even if it helped to prevent diseases in their baby, while only 48 per cent saying they would want it. Three-quarters of those surveyed also believed that these technologies would exacerbate the divide between the haves and the have-nots, concluding that if expensive brain chips became available, only the wealthy could afford them.

Here's the conundrum. We already augment our bodies in many ways. Think of heart pacemakers, plastic surgery, Cochlear hearing implants and bionic eyes. Future options include body suits to enable paraplegics to walk, neuro-prosthetic brain chip implants to reduce depression, brain–computer interfaces enabling us to control household devices through thought alone, and internal nano-devices that fight cancer cells.

So where will we draw our ethical line in the sand with regard to technological enhancements of our bodies? If we believe physical implants already cross that line, then we may have to think even more carefully when gene editing becomes commonplace.

> Genetic engineering will be the Pandora's Box of the mid 21st century.

Genetic engineering will be the Pandora's Box of the mid 21st century. Until recently, gene editing was too expensive and complex, although a technology called CRISPR (Clustered Regularly Interspaced Short Palindromic Repeats) is now up to 99 per cent cheaper and can often be implemented in days, rather than years.[10] CRISPR allows scientists to edit live cells, which will enable them to eliminate HIV, herpes, and hundreds of genetic diseases such as cystic fibrosis.

We may eventually reduce the incidence of chromosome abnormalities that create disorders such as Down syndrome. Such advances raise significant ethical dilemmas. Should we be 'playing

God' in these areas or should we leave well enough alone? If we do decide to intervene, the long-term health benefits will be far-reaching. And they can be expected to extend our children's lifespan to well over a century, assuming they would choose this.

Immortality sounds preposterous to most of us at this time in history, although we can already live forever in artificial ways. MIT Media Lab and Ryerson University have announced a collaborative venture exploring what is termed 'augmented eternity'.[11] Your Intelligent Assistant, or IA, can maintain your social media feed and online life after you physically die. Haunting from beyond the grave will take on a whole new dimension. Your IA would update your information on social media according to new online experiences and circumstances.

We can already exist anywhere, at any time. In 2D video form, we can appear on multiple screens worldwide, now or in the future. Three-dimensional virtual reality (VR) takes the use of stored images a step further. Concerts have already been organised in which a 3D VR representation of a deceased singer performs 'live' on stage.

A further step towards immortality may involve your Intelligent Assistant being implanted in a humanoid entity after your physical body dies. In essence, an artificial copy of your brain would be transplanted into this robotic body. The humanoid would then continue to live in a way that reflected your personality, habits, interests and ethics.

Not only will vastly improved medical support dramatically extend our lifespan, but future technologies will also make that longer life much easier. While washing machines and fridges made 20th century living less onerous, technological innovations of the mid 21st century will revolutionise the performance of everyday tasks.

TECHNOLOGY THAT IMPROVES THE HUMAN CONDITION

Many of us dreamed of having a superpower when we were children. I always wanted to fly. Perhaps you fancied having superhuman strength. If that was the case, then your dream is well on its way to becoming achievable. The RoboGlove[12] has been refined from a robot that works on board the International Space Station. Known as Robonaut, or R2 for short, it takes on tasks that are dangerous for humans.

From this ongoing development project we now have a robotic glove that can be worn by anyone who manipulates objects with their hands. The technology, developed jointly by NASA and General Motors, doubles the strength of the wearer's grip while minimising tendon and muscular damage.

Telepresence robots[13] will reframe what it means to operate physical tools in a specific location. Think of the surgeon in a London hospital who operates on a patient in Kenya through remote robotic manipulation, or the tourist who controls a robot that is physically located on Mars, without leaving the comfort of their own lounge room on Earth.

Until now, remote experiences have generally been channelled through a two-dimensional flat screen, for example using Skype or other forms of video conferencing. The three-dimensional manipulation of telepresence robots will introduce an entirely new realm in online service. Activities that require a 3D presence might one day be performed by anyone, anywhere. Operating a basic robot, an Indonesian horticulturist might monitor forest replanting in Australia. French educators might teach children in Afghanistan.

All of the different enhancements in our children's future will be synchronised in the vast Internet of Things (IoT).[14] Their fitness tracker will be able to connect with their fridge and adjust the food purchases required for their nutritional intake after determining their fitness levels. Their apartment will constantly adjust thermostat settings and lighting when they enter or exit a room. Hotel rooms will automatically reset to each guest's personal preferences, including the artworks on the walls and the lighting in the bathroom.

Many other technologies will support everyday life. Here are some that our children will be using in the future. Many are already in early application.

Personal life

◊   Their Intelligent Assistant will organise everyday tasks such as meal preparation, clothing choice and payment of bills.

◊   An Artificial Intelligence medical monitor will program their wearable devices to encourage optimum nutrition and exercise.

◊   Machine writing software will complete any writing tasks, including that difficult letter to a friend to whom they need to apologise for their behaviour at last night's party.

◊   Translation devices will help them to communicate with people of different cultures, saving the countless hours needed to learn a new language.

The workplace

◊   Typing will be very 20th century. Voice recognition software, iris movement sensors and gesture-based technology will revolutionise the recording of information. Will handwriting be necessary? Only if you enjoy calligraphy.

◊   In education, software will accurately mark a student's assignment and offer suggestions for further improvement in the next assignment.

◊   Use of exoskeletons will allow anyone to lift heavy objects even in tight spaces.

◊   3D visualisation glasses will be used in low safety environments to detect hidden dangers, for example on rock faces or around corners.

◊   Wearable technology will monitor a person's mental and physical responses while performing a task, and provide warnings and time signals to improve performance.

Travel

◊   The traffic accident rate is projected to drop by 90 per cent once most vehicles are autonomous, making life on the road much safer.

◊   The route taken by our children's driverless vehicle, and the music it plays while they are on the journey, may be partly determined by their mobile phone's face recognition software, which will even detect their mood as they approach the vehicle.

◊   3D virtual reality systems will allow remote attendance at meetings. If they cannot make a meeting themselves, their Intelligent Assistant may attend in their place, whether on-screen or in humanoid form.

Despite the many benefits of technological innovation, we have a deep historical fear of the machine overlord, and we have often fought against it. In early 19th century England the Luddites vandalised factory machinery they believed threatened the traditional livelihood of craft workers. The transition from horses to motorcars was another disruptive era. By the mid 21st century robots will have taken over many human activities and radically transformed our society.

Technological advances do have a few strings attached. The issue of privacy raises concerns among many people, and with good reason. Someone

> We have a deep historical fear of the machine overlord.

27

somewhere knows just about everything about you and your life, from the exact route you drive to work to the items you purchase to all your online activity. The genie has already escaped from the privacy bottle.

There are few easy answers to ensuring your privacy, but think carefully before you share your personal details, especially online. Most online competitions are designed expressly to collect those details. There is merit in paying a technician to scour all your devices, including your phone, for bugs. On the other hand, consider the benefits of this open availability to data. When that ambulance arrives at your accident scene, you may be kept alive because the paramedics can instantly access your medical history.

Artificial intelligence will give our children lots of cognitive competition. By the early 2030s, AI computers will probably be intellectually far superior to humans. A few years later, they will be thousands of times more advanced. The benefits might be unlimited, although what will happen when AI surpasses our children's brain capacity? Will HI (Human Intelligence) need to be boosted in some way?

AUGMENTING OUR CHILDREN'S INTELLIGENCE

AI has already achieved some impressive feats, with IBM's Watson winning the *Jeopardy!* TV quiz show and Google's DeepMind becoming world champion at playing the board game Go. This does not mean that machines can 'think'. It simply means that they have vast processing power, which is not the same thing. However, human intelligence is not presently keeping pace with that AI power. Our physical brains have taken many millennia to slowly adjust naturally to changing circumstances. HI develops incrementally, AI exponentially.

TALKING WITH THE NEXT GENERATION

WHEN THEY SAY

'The robots are going to take over the world.'

SOME RESPONSES YOU MIGHT OFFER

'While nothing is perfect, there are lots of safeguards being built into the technology that we develop. **Humans are in charge, and they are always likely to be.** The trouble is that most science fiction movies make the robots look like they are dangerous, and want to take over the world. On the contrary, robots are likely to keep improving our lives.'

'**The technology will work with us, not against us.** Artificial intelligence devices will do the tedious work that is presently a waste of our human talents (such as filling in paperwork) and leave us to apply our creativity in many more interesting ways.'

'**Future technologies will help you to become almost superhuman.** Your IAs (Intelligent Assistants) will keep you more organised; wearable devices will monitor your health and fitness levels; your body strength will be augmented with special gloves and body suits; your thinking will control many of the devices in your life. It is likely to be an extraordinary time.'

One scenario that is often proposed by science fiction writers is a future in which AI entities become a superior species, at least intellectually. The more likely scenario is that our children will continue to take advantage of the technology, whether or not it can calculate faster than they can. Already cars drive us faster than we can run, and machines can lift much heavier loads than we can. Our children will not necessarily need to match future technologies intellectually. They just need to use them to improve their own circumstances.

If our children decide to boost their brain power, they will have several options. A brain chip called a neuro-prosthetic may be implanted in people who are suffering from neurological damage caused by strokes or concussion.[15] This may eventually lead to brain chips that boost human intelligence and memory capacity. Bio-hacking involves engineering the body and mind to dramatically improve functionality. Ray Kurzweil talks of nanobots made from DNA strands that can be injected into the brain to connect your conscious brain to the internet.[16]

> Drones can be piloted by a controller's mind.

Wearable devices such as the SmartCap[17] monitor brainwave patterns through an attached electroencephalogram (EEG) device. This provides users with a regular update on their level of concentration, and is used in the mining industry and office environments in several countries.

With Brain Computer Interface (BCI) technology[18], we control many devices with our thinking. Amputees can move a complex robot arm, a quadriplegic can operate a wheelchair, a drone can be piloted — all by a controller's mind alone.[19]

More complex BCI systems involve implanting electrodes inside the human skull. In current trials the user's brain signals are recorded through a cable screwed into their skull and sent to a large signal processor nearby. These models are bulky and require delicate brain operations that are not for the faint-hearted. We have a long way to go before we can guarantee the safety of such an implant.

BCIs already allow humans to send limited decoded messages to each other through the power of thought.[20] The mobile phone is probably the quintessential contemporary technological device, and its refinements over the next decade are likely to reflect these neuro-advances. The iPhone 18 may allow us to transmit our thoughts to another phone with a surgically implanted neural device. We might need to watch those random thoughts we have as we walk down the street.

There is naturally some reticence about physically delving too deeply into the brain, given that it is at the private core of who we are. However, if an implantable neuro-prosthetic could restore your memory in old age, would you dismiss the option? Would you decline to be given a new heart if your old one malfunctioned? Most people would welcome the opportunity to extend the quality and duration of their life with that transplant. Is the brain all that different?

Imagine the enhanced lives that could be within reach for paraplegics and quadriplegics, and the support that BCIs would provide for those who suffer from brain-acquired injuries. Think of the benefits for aged care if those neuro-prosthetics reduce the ravages of Alzheimer's or other brain-degenerative illnesses.

The hybrid humans of the mid 21st century will be healthier and more intelligent than any of their forebears. These possibilities will challenge our children to rethink how to engage in a meaningful life. One of the most significant components of human life is the work we pursue each day. How will a hybrid human engage in this aspect of their life in the future? We'll explore work's fascinating possibilities in chapter 3.

CHAPTER 3

All in a day's work: redefining future employment

WHAT IT'S ABOUT

Work environments will experience dramatic changes in the next 20 years. What type of employment will be offered to today's children? What skills will they need in the workspace of the future? Will work as we know it even exist? This chapter reviews some of the core issues relating to these futuristic options, and begins by proposing that work has a positive future.

#worktransformation #workpluslife #robotworkers
#consciouscapitalism #workless

WHAT'S HAPPENING WITH WORK TODAY?

What do you want to be when you grow up? Children must roll their eyes at the question, given today's increasingly flexible workplace. So what career revolution awaits them in the mid 21st century? Here is one scenario that you don't often read about in the media: many of our children may enjoy exciting work that makes a positive contribution to the planet.

Given the dystopian predictions of the robot-ravaged future of work, that sounds hard to believe, doesn't it? Let's face it, if there is one issue that is overwhelmed by negativity more than any other, it is the world of future employment. Even today, all eyes are turned to the 5 to 10 per cent unemployment rate in most countries, and we must absolutely give support to that minority. However, few journalists write about the 90 to 95 per cent employment rate.

Optimistic future work is one possible scenario, although some transformational thinking will be needed before we create it. Let's start by asking what we even mean by work. Are we referring to paid employment, stay-at-home family support, part-time volunteering, caring for the less fortunate in our communities? If it's all of these, then we will never be short of work. Social justice and philanthropy options are discussed later in the book, so here we'll focus on paid employment.

Flexible roles and rapid transitions between jobs are becoming commonplace. Casual employees, independent contractors, part-time workers, and remote workers and providers in the 'gig economy' are elements of this variable world of work. Some will need to work in these situations because they have no other choice. Many others will choose to do so because they love the independence and flexibility.

Agile workers who are quick to respond to change will thrive in this fast-paced environment. In the new world of work, we will move on from the traditional notion that we each have a single full-time employee role for our entire working lives. In 2016, 86 per cent of new jobs in Australia were part-time.[1] By May 2016, the number of self-employed people in the UK nearly matched the number who worked in the public service.[2] More than 33 per cent of the US workforce is presently engaged in some form of freelance work.[3]

Most of our children will do many forms of work during their lifetime. This is good news for the under-20s, who generally recoil from the thought of remaining in a single work position for 40 or more years. They have watched their parents endure long work hours in an unloved job, and the prospect does not interest them in the least. They want work to be an inspiration and a core component of a quality life.

> They have watched their parents endure long work hours in an unloved job, and the prospect does not interest them in the least.

My niece Kate, now 33, has already worked in 11 jobs since leaving university. She's smart, sassy and an excellent senior HR advisor. Her premise? When an organisation has fully benefited from your skills, and you have learned as much as you can from being there, it's time to move on. Her husband Owen, an engineer, has held six jobs over the same time period.

This workplace adaptability changes how we can help support our children into employment. We won't be preparing them for one job. We will be preparing them for many. In times past, parents would ask: What sort of work will be available for my children in the future? While this question has merit, it also indicates a focus on a single job.

A more insightful question would be: What capabilities will help my children to find employment in an unknown future? Capabilities such as adaptability and critical thinking will help our children to adjust to rapid change. Our quick-fix mentality searches for an immediate answer to the first question, in the hope that we can then direct them towards one profession. The second question prepares children more broadly for whatever might transpire. That question will be addressed further in chapters 4, 5 and 6 when we clarify some of the capabilities that children will need.

What capabilities will help my children to find employment in an unknown future?

Predicting the world of work in 20 or more years from now is challenging, given the vast number of events that may occur between now and then. It is akin to forecasting the sharemarket in two decades from now. Good luck with that. However, trends can provide a reasonable indicator of the near future of work. For example, analyses of American workers through the first years of the 21st century show that most of the jobs growth has occurred in what is called interaction work.

This is when we require the highest level of human-to-human interface, such as with doctors and teachers. In *Humans Are Underrated*, Geoff Colvin writes that those types of jobs increased in the United States by 4.8 million between 2001 and 2009, at a time when production jobs decreased by 2.7 million.[4] He continues: 'The biggest increases by far have been in education and health services, which have more than doubled as a percentage of total jobs; professional and business services, up by 80%; and leisure and hospitality, up about 50%'. Welcome to a human-centric workplace in which personal and social skills are critical.

The conclusions from a Regional Australia Institute analysis[5] reflect the majority of studies done around the planet on the future of work. According to this report, the most sought-after workers in 2030 and beyond will be high-touch (trades and construction), high-care (nursing, childcare and wellness industries) and high-tech (all things digital). They are jobs that robots cannot do ... for now.

CREATING THE NEW WORLD OF WORK

Let's push some limits here and romanticise about a future of work that is enticing, exciting and outright inspiring. Imagine that everyone woke up each morning delighted to be heading off to a day of productive contribution. At the end of the day, they would express gratitude for the honour of being involved in their labour. Don't laugh. Some people already experience their work in this way. I'm one of them.

If everyone did engage with their work in this way, just imagine the levels of productivity we would see. What difference would it make to problems such as depression? How much would the national economy improve over a period of time? The word 'revolutionary' springs to mind, doesn't it? Unfortunately, in the beautiful mess of daily work, we have come to a point where for too many it is simply a chore rather than a contribution. For the sake of our children's work future, let's create a different work narrative. We want Charlie and every other child to shift their mindframe from seeing work as a job to seeing it as a contribution.

In *The Little Prince*, Antoine de Saint-Exupéry wrote, 'If you want to build a ship, don't drum up people together to collect wood and don't assign them tasks and work, but rather teach them to long for the endless immensity of the sea'. That longing is more likely to be found when we explore three significant factors.

1. Work Plus Life

We can no longer separate work from life. It's not a work–life balance we need, given the present imbalances in which work overwhelms life. What we need is a Work Plus Life experience in which each part is enjoyed in association with the other. Gen Ys and Gen Zs are already making choices that reflect this Work Plus Life.

US gerontologist Ken Dychtwald, co-author of *Age Wave*, suggests that many of today's under-30s live in flexible seven-year work cycles, rather than a linear one-job, 45-year pattern.[6, 7] For six and a half years, they learn and earn in a specific profession, and for six months they 'retire' to pursue a lifetime ambition. This might involve the study of tango in Argentina or the support of orang-utans in Borneo. Some may take seven years to complete this cycle, some two years, but the principle stands.

On their return from their tango party, they begin another seven-year cycle, sometimes in an entirely different profession, and they work through these cycles until they are 94 years old. It will become a form of perpetual career transition. Retirement, in any case, will be a very different concept in the 2050s. Governments won't be able to afford to pay pensions by then, even though people will be living and working longer.

When I mention this seven-year cycle to older adults, some throw up their hands in horror. This is why young people can't afford a house, they complain. They don't know how to settle down and create a long-term career. While there is certainly much to be said for the benefits of stable saving and investment, these older critics may be caught in a 20th century mode of thinking. This is the one that goes: Work hard, buy a house, stay in one job for decades while paying off that house, and when you retire, enjoy your life. This is a Dickensian perspective, especially if life enjoyment is delayed until near the end of your life.

2. Impacts of technology

Of course technology will impact on the workplace. It always has. Will there be mass sackings, layoffs and redundancies? Yes there will, as there always have been. The history of automation indicates that while technology often replaces humans, those same humans usually—although not always—move on to other work positions.

The oft-quoted prediction that up to 50 per cent of jobs will be displaced by technology within 10 years needs to be treated with caution. It's a simplistic statement. Robotics will expose us to many shades of grey. For example, these technologies are very good at highly specific tasks, although not so good at adapting to lots of different tasks at once. For now at least, humans are much better than robots when flexibility is needed. Robots won't often replace whole jobs. They will replace segments of jobs.

A McKinsey Global Institute study[8] found that only around 5 per cent of jobs would be entirely replaced by robots, although about 45 per cent of all activities at work might be automated. Based on technologies that exist now, the study estimated that AI might replace around one-third of all work in about 60 per cent of occupations.

Any well-run business looks for improved efficiencies in everyday production, so it's understandable that it will consider the return on some degree of automation. We can hardly blame them in the short term for resorting to robotics. Some would be out of business if they didn't. Practices that compromise human society are another matter. In the most extreme case, robots have taken over all the work, and no one has a job any longer because wages are too expensive. Even now we are seeing a race to the bottom as manufacturers compete with each other to produce cheaper goods.

> The oft-quoted prediction that up to 50 per cent of all jobs will be displaced by technology within 10 years needs to be treated with caution.

In *The Rise of the Robots*,[9] Martin Ford imagines, tongue-in-cheek, a future in which friendly aliens take over the planet. All they want to do is work for free. At first, businesses are suspicious of their motives, but they very soon delight in this unexpected free labour force. Unfortunately, they need to lay off all of their human workers ... but hey, it's all about the financial bottom line.

For a time, these businesses make a huge profit, given there are no wages to pay. Very soon, though, their profits plummet because their former employees and the many other unemployed have no money to pay for the business's goods and services. At that point, the entire economic system as we know it today simply collapses.

A more probable scenario is that the machines will blend into the human workplace and make many careers more productive, and perhaps even enjoyable. Robots will assume all the disagreeable drudgery that takes up so much of our valuable time. This will allow us to better utilise our human skills and create more productive careers. We need to humanise work and leave the tedious tasks to the machines.

3. A new social understanding of work

At parties you will often be asked, 'So what do you do with your life?' There is usually an expectation that you will then describe your career in some detail. I sometimes reply, 'I love learning, I travel a lot, I enjoy doing social justice work, I work on becoming a better human being'. Sometimes this elicits a confused stare. I obviously haven't conformed to social expectations by talking about some form of high-paying and interesting job.

And that's the thing. We need to change the perception that what we do (in our professional life) is who we are. It is as though our work has become our life, and whatever we do to earn a living represents our life. In *Why the Future Is Workless*, Tim Dunlop argues, 'This centrality of work to modern existence and to our everyday understanding of what it means to be human is so complex that we rarely examine it, but we really need to'.[10]

We sure do. The dilemma is that whenever we don't have any work, we may be considered as somehow a lesser human being. This perspective will need to be fully reconsidered over the next few decades. Many of our children will be living flexible lives in which they weave in and out of work. Less employment will mean something very different in the years ahead. Without a collective reframe on this attitude, we will end up with a significant number of people who feel as though they have failed in life.

In the 2040 version of work, we will respect those who are not working in a paid permanent position. It will be unusual for someone to have stayed in one core job for life. Community esteem will more likely be earned by those who have flexibly and who have successfully balanced their work and life.

If the shame of not having a job persists in the future, we will never move forward to a more respectful and optimistic attitude towards less employment. Perhaps we need a new descriptor for someone who is not fully working. Possible definitions include *transition*, *inbetween*, *work vacation* or *part employed*. Changing the language will achieve nothing, however, if we don't reframe our thinking about what it means to not be fully 'working'.

Old thinking habits die hard. Censorious labels such as 'dole bludger' and 'lazy' are too easily associated with the less employed. Perhaps one in 40 people don't want to work and would choose to live for free off the tax-paying public. We must not associate the wide range of other, less employed people with this very small group. Most are actively searching for work, or are in transition, or are enjoying a three-month break after six intensive years of work.

When I discuss this 21st century mindframe with corporate CEOs, some respond frankly that many people need an incentive to keep working … and the best inducement is the fear of *not* having any work. That may suit a full-work non-flexible 20th century society, but not one in which work is in shorter supply. Instead, let's steadily develop a mindframe about work that reflects the flexibility of life today, and that respects everyone. If we make the effort, this might just support workplaces that help create an even better society.

WORKPLACES THAT CREATE A BETTER SOCIETY

The conscious capitalism practised by Toms Shoes[11] has two worthwhile outcomes: a thriving business and a more sustainable society. The business is based on a 50:50 model: when you buy a pair of shoes from their online store, they will donate another pair to a needy person in a developing country, while taking care that any small businesses in that region are not financially compromised.

41

In some parts of the world, children without shoes are not allowed to attend school, so these shoes can change lives.

Critics have questioned the business model, asking how it can be profitable to double production for a smaller margin. There is the twist. Businesses that adopt such an approach often attract significant extra custom. Socially aware customers often resonate with a 50:50 business that supports others, and will reciprocate by buying from them.

So what other types of workplaces can we see up ahead that might help create a better society? One example is companies that provide paid time off for employees to volunteer with local charities. Diabetes drug giant Novo Nordisk offers 80 hours of paid time off for volunteering each year. Deloitte provides unlimited paid time for volunteering.[12]

The Google Crisis Response team offers essential services such as Person Finder and Public Alerts during times of disaster.[13] Companies that provide these opportunities rate highly in employee satisfaction surveys. A core human value is to support others in need, and workplaces such as these give employees the opportunity to practise this value.

Conscious capitalism[14] has massive merit. Its supporters contend that our economic systems have contributed to global environmental problems and the gross imbalance between rich and poor. They propose a different model of capitalism that protects the environment and benefits all people, and notably all workers.

What are the benefits of conscious capitalism for business owners? There are many. It authentically aligns business and ethical goals. They can demonstrate that they care deeply about their employees and their customers, rather than just their shareholders. They don't even have to choose between employees and shareholders. Conscious capitalism organisations outperform the market, some by a factor of more than 10.[15] So the shareholders will love the idea anyway.

A study paper from PwC called 'The Future of Work: A Journey to 2022'[16] outlines three possible future work scenarios. In the Blue World, mega-organisations just get bigger, with scant regard paid to the principles of

> Conscious capitalism organisations outperform the market, some by a factor of more than 10.

conscious capitalism or individual preferences. In the Orange World, organisations break down into smaller collaborative networks, with work specialisation dominating the world economy. The Green World features companies that care about people, with social responsibility and sustainable practices high on their agenda.

In which work world would you prefer to engage? Blue, Orange or Green? In which one would you prefer your children to work? We have some choice in this matter. Most people prefer not to work with an organisation that has no respect for individual employees. As consumers too, we prefer to buy goods and services from companies that support their employees, and this economic pressure in itself can drive organisational change. Consider the B Team.[17]

With luminaries such as Richard Branson, Arianna Huffington and Muhammad Yunus among its driving forces, this initiative is committed to supporting a better way of doing business. Why do they call it the B Team? In business parlance, Plan A describes the practice of placing profit before purpose. So Plan B places purpose before profit, with business driving social, environmental and economic benefits for all. Time and again it has been demonstrated that a Plan B organisation will also be more profitable.

Is this the sort of workplace that will appeal to young people in the future? Another PwC paper titled 'Engaging and Empowering Millennials'[18] reviews some of the work practices that young workers would prefer. This is more than just a frivolous wish list; it aligns directly with Plan B practices. Suggested initiatives include: create a more flexible work environment; fully leverage technology; create innovative programs around compensation, rewards and career decisions; build a sense of community; and invest time, resources and energy to listen and stay connected with your people. This sounds like a decent description of a desirable society.

By 2025, Gen Zs will make up about 31 per cent of the workforce.[19] With such weight of numbers, their needs and intentions will drive many workplace changes. Gen Zs prefer to work with organisations that respect them and invest in social capital both locally and globally. They want collaboration over authoritarianism. The full spectrum of work conditions determines whether they will remain with the organisation and contribute productively. The question remains: in spite of these many enticing possibilities for future work, what if our children end up working less, or even have no work at all?

DEALING WITH A WORK-LESS SOCIETY

Perhaps our greatest concern is that young people will be unable to generate a viable income in their adult years. If those pesky robots do supplant them, then how will our children derive an income to pay for goods and services? Let's start with a proposal that will drive most capitalists mad: a work-less society may have much merit. Note that I said 'work-less', not 'no work at all'. A total loss of paid work would certainly raise some issues. At that point we'd need to develop an entirely new economic system.

Take a deep breath, and think two decades ahead…which is not easy, of course. In times ahead, we may not need as much income to enjoy our daily lives. Molecular assemblers and 3D printers may produce most goods so cheaply that we would require very little money to pay for them. Even houses and apartments would be 3D printed for a much lower cost. Our earnings may be supplemented through some future version of the 'gig economy', in which our entrepreneurial flair would determine the amount of extra money we wished to make.

Less work may have multiple benefits, given that many people don't even like their job. The reasons for this can vary from a lack of purpose and meaning, to a dislike of the boss or the long hours, to the knowledge that they are only doing it for the money. Full-time employment sometimes even becomes time and a half, with workers engaged in massive overtime that compromises their physical and mental health, let alone their precious time with their family.

Ask your friends what they would do if they won Lotto. Most—although not all—will admit that their first action would be to resign from their work. This indicates that their wage is one of the main reasons for continuing with the job. This beautiful mess of a workplace will never become a joyful part of life if money is the key driver. Surely we want our children to see work as a contribution, rather than just as a vehicle to pay for other enjoyable experiences outside work.

> A work-less society may have much merit.

If money becomes an issue for our children in the future—and that's very understandable—there will be many flexible options available to them. Here are some that already exist, and are likely to continue up ahead:

◊ Starting a small side business in the gig economy. This might involve Fiverr, TaskRabbit, Uber or another flexible organisation that encourages part-time initiative.

◊ Selling some products on eBay. Just look at a site called Terapeak and you will find all kinds of sales information about nearly every product imaginable. If you're after a model of how to set up your own version of eBay, look no further than Alibaba, the world's biggest e-commerce group.

◊ Renting out anything that is superfluous to your needs. This might mean placing your apartment's spare bedroom on Airbnb, hiring out your driveway for parking if you live near a sports stadium, or renting out your appliances or tools when you don't need them.

◊ At least six countries are already exploring the possibility of a Universal Basic Income, by which every adult is paid a small monthly wage. In localised settings, this concept often works. Full national implementation would be a bureaucratic nightmare in the early stages. If such a program is ever introduced, it will at least cover your food bills.

Bill Gates has proposed that we tax robots that are doing future work.[20] This idea could be of great interest to governments looking for ways to maintain their public services. As a variation, our children might one day lease out their own robot that is programmed to do the work they would normally do themselves.

Here's the reality behind all of these ideas: there will be infinite financial possibilities up ahead, and this will challenge us to rethink the concept of earning a wage from a single full-time job.

While money will be uppermost in some people's minds, perhaps an even more important consideration is our wellbeing and happiness. A work-less society may give our children the opportunity to experience the Work Plus Life scenario.

People sometimes argue that without lots of money they wouldn't be able to afford any leisure experiences. An annual world tour, or even the family sojourn at an expensive theme park, might be hard to support. But there is an endless list of fulfilling activities that cost very little. Reading, listening to music, having a coffee with friends, playing with the kids in a park, going for a jog—all have huge value for our mental and physical wellness.

Aristotle talked of *eudaimonia*, a Greek word that translates as 'human flourishing'. This flourishing is derived from experiences that fulfil the soul and, by focusing on the human good, steadily enable you to become a better person. Perhaps *eudaimonia* will become the trend of the 2040s.

TALKING WITH THE NEXT GENERATION

WHEN THEY SAY

'I won't have any work in the future.'

SOME RESPONSES YOU MIGHT OFFER

'**There will still be lots of work to do.** It will just be different from today's world, and will include flexible options such as part-time work, contract work and the 'gig' economy. It's likely that you will sometimes create your own work opportunities, rather than just waiting for someone to give you a 'job'. Your initiative will then drive your success in that work.'

'There probably won't be as much work in factories any more, but **the services that directly support people — such as health and education — will need more employees for a long time yet.** Learning how to respect other people, and to really care about them, will be a critical skill in most people's work future.'

'**One secret to making yourself more employable in the future is to develop your "enterprise skills".** These will always be needed, no matter what new jobs might be created. Here are some examples of these skills: Be a critical thinker. Know how to be an innovative worker. Understand how to use digital technologies that would benefit an employer. Learn how to communicate respectfully with your co-workers.'

This is not an argument for laziness. It is a challenge to reconsider what it means to live a life of depth and purpose, rather than one where the struggle to earn an income overwhelms the joy of being alive. Paid work can fill up to one-third of the sum total of hours in our lives, and often more. Surely we want our children to free themselves from the trap of endless soul-destroying work.

The upcoming robot workplace revolution might offer them the opportunity to reimagine what it means to live a balanced life. Given so many positive scenarios, where do we start in preparing today's children for this astonishing new world of work?

PREPARING CHILDREN FOR THE NEW WORLD OF WORK

Think back to when you were 12 years old. Did you know then what work you would be doing today? It's possible that a few may have had some idea, although it is unlikely many did. It's even more improbable for today's children as they ponder the mid 21st century. When you are discussing work futures with them, there is little merit in asking them what they want to do when they grow up. Charlie is 12 years old today, but the world will be dramatically different by the time he is 20.

Instead, ask him *why* he wants to be involved in something, and what deeply drives him. Then ask him *how* he might accomplish this. And only then perhaps ask him *what* profession or work experience might help him to create that solution.

Expand his mind about options that would excite him. Introduce him to a wide variety of people in different professions. Discuss the points raised in this chapter. Invite him to think about how work will be even more flexible a decade from now. Ask him which work world — Blue, Orange or Green — would most appeal to him, and then encourage him to justify his choice. Explain the merits of a roboticised work-less future, and help him to keep an open mind about the possibilities.

Remember that every child is a unique individual. Some may be destined for the medical field and work in a large hospital; others will delight in selling their artwork on eBay. Be careful not to live your life vicariously through them. Perhaps you always wanted to be a doctor but didn't have the opportunity. That is not a good enough reason to impose your choice on them. Give respectful advice, while making no demands. If they end up suffering through years of study followed by a heartbreaking struggle in an unsuitable profession, then your parenting relationship may be compromised.

Develop a Best Fit series of life pathways for each young person. Different children will respond to different approaches. We need to help each of them to discover their own way to contribute to society. How do we do that? One powerful tool is to encourage them to develop a life portfolio from an early age. This will be full of real-life experiences, a collation of what they have accomplished that will help clarify what appeals to them.

> Encourage children to develop a life portfolio from an early age.

This portfolio is not something that can be written in a few days. It will take them years to authentically achieve what is on their list, so help them start early. Ten-year-olds can begin a portfolio, as long as the purpose for doing so is clarified. Throughout their teenage years, they would steadily collate their academic results, creative projects and sporting successes, as well as good deeds and other exciting life experiences. Think creatively about the process used for recording what they have achieved.

Rather than just pieces of paper in a plastic folder, their portfolio might include short video interviews, verbal testimonials and social media links to images of their work. As long as security measures are in place, they might draw together all of the material in one visual spectacle on their own website.

In the near future, that portfolio may prove as important as a university degree. More CEOs already place strong emphasis on a prospective employee's up-to-date portfolio of applicable skills and experiences. Does this mean a six-year university degree will lose relevance? No, it doesn't. We will still need to know that professionals are well qualified to practise their craft. Accreditation is critical. You would not want an operation from a brain surgeon who consulted YouTube videos for instruction.

Earlier in this chapter we posed a powerful question: What capabilities will help children to find employment in a future we can't easily predict? In Part II we explore three critical capabilities that directly respond to that question. We begin, in chapter 4, with *adaptive agility*.

PART II

ESSENTIAL CAPABILITIES

CHAPTER 4

Life in the fast lane: developing their adaptive agility

WHAT IT'S ABOUT

Adaptive agility will become a prized capability for our children in rapidly changing times. This chapter explores how they can adjust their thinking to welcome uncertainty and develop a more peaceful soul in the rush of life. We begin by considering the filters that will be needed to cope with information overload.

#adaptiveagility #filters #neuroscience #perseverance #mindfulness

FILTERING THE OVERLOAD

Some legends are of dubious authenticity, although we love to imagine they really happened. One of my favourites involves a 19th century explorer marching relentlessly through the African jungle towards a distant mountain. In his impatience to reach his destination, he used every means to force his native bearers to go faster. With threats and inducements he drove them on through the dense undergrowth.

But as they neared the base of the mountain, the bearers abruptly stopped and sat down, and no amount of threats or promises of extra pay would induce them to move. When the explorer demanded to know why, they replied simply, 'Because we are waiting for our souls to catch up'.

Perhaps we need to wait for our souls to catch up. The accelerating rate of change in work and life contrasts markedly with the steady linear change of the past two millennia. It is as though God is holding down the fast-forward button on a heavenly remote control, and today is pointing it directly at us.

The vast proliferation of global data is one illustration of this accelerating change. In *Critical Path*, R. Buckminster Fuller[1] conjectured that everything known by earlier civilisations up to the birth of Christ might be considered as one unit of knowledge. It took about 1500 years for that amount of knowledge to double. The next doubling occurred within 250 years, and the next before we had reached the year 1900.

By 1950, it had grown to about sixteen units of knowledge. Extrapolating from this, the world has now amassed over one million units. Today, this endless data is measured in what are called zettabytes. Around 2010, total online data had reached 1 zettabyte, which is equal to one thousand billion billion bytes or '1' followed by 21 zeros. By 2013, it had grown to 4 zettabytes.[2] By 2020, it will reach about forty-four zettabytes. By 2030, it is calculated to grow to 1400 zettabytes.

Here's a reality check. While those numbers might sound overwhelming, there is nothing new to information overload. The Library of Celsus in Anatolia, Turkey,[3] completed in AD 125, stored over 12 000 scrolls. Even now, the thought of reading so many texts is a daunting prospect. While the amount of online data today is quantum degrees larger, there has always been too much information in the world for any single person to absorb. This was as true in the 2nd and the 12th century as it is the 21st century.

The issue is not so much the sheer amount of information in our lives today. As Clay Shirky famously put it, 'It's not information overload. It's filter failure'.[4] More effective filters make it easier to cope with overwhelming information. Think about filters as a magic pair of glasses we use to find what we are looking for. These glasses save us from having to search through the entire haystack for the needle we seek. Filters curate what is worthwhile and important for us.

Filters fall into two categories: external and internal. External filters do the screening for us. Spam email filters hide what we don't want to see, while news feeds and aggregators collate

> More effective filters make it easier to cope with overwhelming information.

what we do want to see. If you love to spend 10 minutes each day perusing topics of interest, the Flipboard app is one example of an effective news feed.

David Weinberger[5] describes the internet as the biggest crowd anyone has ever seen. And we have unprecedented access to the collective wisdom of that crowd. I love watching movies, and I've yet to be disappointed by a new release that has a crowd rating above 90 per cent. When 15-year-olds are thinking of buying some music or a new computer game, or watching a YouTube video, they start by checking out the online ratings. They know the crowd is smarter than any one of them and will help them choose. Do they still make their own choices? Of course they do. Can millions of people help them make a wiser choice? They certainly can.

Children's internal filters are activated when they ask a question such as, 'Will this information serve any lasting purpose for me?' Internal filtering helps them feel less overwhelmed. Part of coping with rapid change is to deftly sidestep what is not relevant to them. They will know they can do this when they deliberately avoid drifting through their endlessly updated social media. Filtering who they follow is a good start.

Some people complain about the way data consumes their lives. We now need an opposite belief system. Think of this as the best time in human history for accessing knowledge. We own devices that can filter precisely what we need when we need it. Thirty years ago, we had to trudge down to the public library to do it, and there was no guarantee that the book we wanted had been shelved in the right place. Now we take a mobile phone out of our pocket to access the information we need in moments.

Let's turn the entire belief system about rapid change on its head. According to Douglas Thomas and John Seely Brown in *A New Culture of Learning*,[6] we need to embrace change rather than fight it. As they explain, 'It means viewing the future as a set of new possibilities, rather than something that forces us to adjust. It means making the most of a world in motion'. Learning how to filter information will help our children to embrace the endless changes.

As much as anything else, the belief system our children develop about change will determine how adaptive they will be to their future. When two different teenagers are exposed to the same new experience, one may see it as an opportunity, the other as a threat. To help with this, let's show children how to take advantage of the very best resource they have for adapting to change. The secret is to become the architect of their own brain, and to learn how to adjust their own thinking according to changing circumstances.

BECOMING THE ARCHITECT OF THEIR OWN BRAIN

Neuroscience is a complex area, but it can explain many of life's mysteries to children.[7] Why are they sometimes in a bad mood without any apparent reason? How can they adjust more easily to constant changes at school? Why is it so difficult to reason with their parents in their teenage years? Admittedly, they probably won't ever work out that last one. It is their brain that sends positive or negative signals about the changes in their life.[8] Controlling those signals is critical.

This control will depend on whether children believe they can be the architect of their own brain's ongoing development. While they may have been born with a specific brain

> They can be the architect of their own brain's ongoing development.

capacity, they can still influence how it grows and changes. A child's everyday thinking continually shapes who they are, so let's guide them towards taking responsibility for creating those thoughts.

Out of all the information that may change a child's life, this is probably the most critical they will ever implement. Just imagine the difference it would make to children's adaptive agility if they believed in this particular superpower. Yes, it is a superpower, because it can improve how they respond to every different experience for the rest of their lives.

The first step in developing this superpower is to show children how to *self-talk*. Most can master this skill by the age of seven, and sometimes even younger. Place some words in front of them on paper or a screen—perhaps something like, 'This room has white walls'. Ask them to say the words inside their head at normal speaking speed, without moving their lips or making any sound. The words can be repeated several times, until they become aware of how they can control the talk in their own brain. Explain how they can self-talk whenever they are solving a problem.

Here is when you will know this self-talk is working. Think of an occasion when a child approaches you for help. Too often you will find they keep asking you without even thinking about a solution themselves. Then, one auspicious day, they pause before asking you, and you notice that they are self-talking their way through to a solution by themselves. This is the turning point to their learning to control this 'superpower'.

Self-talk can be used in study, in sport, in any social setting. It is when children become aware of their own thoughts and feelings, which allows them to control those thoughts and feelings. They then come to understand that they can take ownership of their actions, and especially their beliefs. The most important of these beliefs is what they think of themselves, and how intelligent they consider themselves to be.

Carol Dweck's concept of the 'Growth Mindset'[9] supports this approach. According to her research, when children believe they can get smarter, they can make choices that help them to improve. Children with a fixed mindset, by contrast, are convinced they cannot change who they are. One of the most heart-breaking experiences for me is to meet with children who are convinced they are a failure, and that nothing can help them to improve.

To turn this around, help them to set small attainable goals. Build up a pattern of working on the goal, and when it is achieved, celebrate it before setting the next goal. Rather than just telling them they are smart, give them consistent feedback on the effort they put into the goal. Children don't think they can immediately improve their intelligence, whereas they know they can control the effort they put into a task.

In *The Brain That Changes Itself*, Norman Doidge[10] helped millions to better understand how to steadily change their own brain. His descriptions of acquired brain injury patients who healed themselves are inspirational. As one patient said in a BBC interview, 'You are not stuck with the brain you were born with. You may be given certain genes but what you do in your life changes your brain. And that's the magic wand'.[11] Anyone who has ever exercised a particular part of their body will understand this. If you have chosen your exercises well, and you consistently implement them, you will eventually feel the positive difference in your body's performance.

While the brain is a complex entity, metaphorically it can be compared to a muscle that requires a constant workout. Based on my experiences as a teacher, I can assure you that a few months of intensive thinking stimulation leads to tangible improvements in most children's verbal and writing skills.

Encourage children to look after their brain as much as they look after their body. We make so much effort to develop awareness in them of their body's needs and their general physical health. An awareness of their brain's functioning and their mental health is just as important. If any parent is serious about exercising their children's brain, then the best time to start is in the early years. The first thousand days of a child's life are critical for brain development, according to a study published by the World Economic Forum.[12]

Their research shows that investing time, money and effort into support before the pre-school stage produces many vital lifelong outcomes. These include better jobs and healthier environments, a higher quality of cognitive functions when they grow up, and greater resilience to mid-life adversities and the challenges of the ageing process such as Alzheimer's. All of these life-altering factors can be influenced before a child turns three years old. It's a no-brainer for society to invest in this age group.

After you have supported them through their infant and early childhood years, you will need to give lots of help to their teenage brain. Just before puberty, they experience a huge boost in brain cell formation. Once they reach puberty, and for five or so years afterwards, they undergo what is called synaptic pruning, when the brain rids itself of unnecessary cells. In effect, their brain is undergoing reconstruction, which explains some of their occasionally aberrant behaviour.

This pruning is an opportune time to shape their brain for the rest of their lives. Teenagers who receive insufficient intellectual stimulation during these years may lose even more of those neurons than normal. Engaging in a variety of enriching learning experiences helps to develop a well-functioning brain as they enter late adolescence.

ADAPTIVE AGILITY IN THEIR EVERYDAY LIVES

While children will enjoy at least some of these new experiences, there will be other changes in their life that appeal to them less. Some experiences will be distinctly uncomfortable, and like many adults, children will often try to avoid them. Let's consider what to do when an unavoidable life event, such as changing schools, is imminent. If your own children have had to go through this experience, then you will know the misery it can cause.

Children may move to a different school because you have changed where you live, or perhaps you have decided that another school will be more suitable for their education. Most commonly, the change occurs when children move up from primary to secondary school. Whatever the reason, this change can create mayhem in a family.

When you first suggested to Charlie that there might be merit in moving to another school, he immediately went into denial. You wondered if he had even heard you when you introduced the option, although you knew this was often the initial stage in changing something in his (or anyone's) life. Over the next couple of weeks, you made further efforts to engage him in dialogue about the option, and he continued to act as though you were talking about someone else. This was the calm before the storm.

After dinner one night, he began to resist forcefully. He had obviously thought it through, and his arguments were persuasive and consistent. You realised this was going to be a drawn-out affair. However, rather than challenging his reasoning, you listened carefully and showed respect for what he had to say.

Through the next month, you cautiously explained a compelling set of benefits to him of moving to the new school. You were smart enough to keep your sales pitch at a low-key level, while offering inducements that would strongly appeal to him. Slowly and surely, Charlie's responses moved from resistance to muted acceptance. Instead of arguing, he began to ask measured questions.

Finally, a brief visit to the school changed the tenor of the conversation, and he became fully involved in the organisation of his move the following year. Later on, you explained to Charlie the process that you had used with him. You had accepted his initial denial, you had listened through his resistance, you had supported him during his slow acceptance of the move, and finally you had celebrated his full involvement in this life-changing option.

Charlie was an excellent thinker for a 12-year-old. In a further conversation, you explained to him that this change process of Denial → Resistance → Acceptance → Involvement would happen throughout his life, and how useful it was to understand when it was happening to him. It didn't take long for an opportunity to appear. As every one of us has discovered, some of life's biggest lessons occur when we are embarrassed by what we do badly. So what was Charlie's humiliating experience?

He had to give a presentation to his class...and it was a disaster. Later, he realised that he simply had not prepared well enough. The other children were obviously not interested in his talk, and his teacher's tentative public feedback to him was a clear signal that he had given a lacklustre performance. It was excruciating.

For a few hours afterwards, Charlie felt mortified, and didn't even think about what went wrong. He was in denial that he had performed badly. That night, he began to resist the feedback he had been given. 'It's not fair,' he protested to himself. 'They expect me to give an adult presentation. But how can I?' This resistance, which focused on blaming everyone except himself, lasted for several days.

Later that week, Charlie revisited his teacher's feedback comments, and slowly recognised that there was no escaping reality: it really had been a poor effort. He started to accept that it had been his own responsibility to prepare the talk properly, and that he had no one to blame but himself. Over the next few weeks, he thought about what he would do better next time. He sought advice from others, including his teacher. He even wrote down what he would do when delivering future presentations.

Charlie had accepted his mediocre effort and was ready to learn from his mistakes. In a conversation with you, he explained what he had learned about himself, and how he would be more aware of it next time he faced a new experience. Smiling quietly to yourself, you felt confident that Charlie's new-found adaptive agility would make his life both more exciting and more effective. His next stage of development would enrich this process further. He would learn how to persevere with everything he did.

ENCOURAGING THEIR PERSEVERANCE

You have to admire Vincent van Gogh's perseverance. He sold just one painting in his lifetime, even though he completed more than 800 before he died. Today the most expensive one is worth more than US$179 million. Another inspiring example of perseverance is Terry Fox, who once ran a marathon every day for 143 days across a large part of Canada. And he accomplished this after having had a leg amputated because of cancer.

Edison reputedly failed 1000 times before inventing the light bulb. Other versions claim there were up to 10 000 failures, so the story obviously grows in the telling. We might settle on a number somewhere in-between. Similar levels of perseverance would certainly help Charlie to cope with all of the changes he will face in his life.

There are many interpretations of perseverance, ranging from persistence to patience, resilience, tenacity, commitment, conscientiousness, drive and focus. They all play a part in the complex human labyrinth of persevering with a task. There is an interesting twist here for our children. Is it possible that they can persevere with a task over a long period of time, yet still adjust quickly to changing circumstances? Adaptive agility and perseverance sometimes appear to be at odds with each other.

On the contrary, it now matters more than ever that children are able to persevere with a task. Being agile with change does not mean that children need to switch rapidly from one activity to another all the time. In that uncertain future world of theirs, that would create an excuse for never persevering with what they were doing.

Too many children today are not persisting with problem-solving in particular, although this lack of commitment is sometimes culturally specific.[13] When children in many Asian countries are given a difficult maths problem in class, they view it as a challenge that needs to be resolved. Even when it is something they have not been taught, many will spend whatever time it takes to find a solution.

> One US study found that American children spend 34 seconds on a difficult task before they begin avoiding it.

In stark contrast, one US study found that American children spend 34 seconds on a difficult task before they begin avoiding it.[14] 'We haven't done this before' or 'How can you expect us to do this?' are common responses. American children are not the only ones who respond in this way. So why are they giving up so quickly?

In a *Huffington Post* article,[15] Tim Elmore offered four reasons why children do not persevere with a task:

◊ Adults make life as convenient as possible for children, so they remove obstacles rather than welcoming them.

◊ Children have an unbalanced view of how to achieve great results. Accustomed to seeing fast-action video highlights of top performers, they rarely get an insight into the countless hours of practice required.

◊ They google an answer for any problem, rather than thinking it through for themselves.

◊ They are too quickly rescued by well-meaning adults, rather than being left to fend for themselves.

Time constraints and the endless rush they generate contribute to this lack of perseverance in children. In some families, there is the daily pressure to get everyone ready to leave for school or other events. Teachers are desperate to complete a crowded curriculum, which results in a sense of rushing through the learning. We are creating a generation of children subjected to constant multiple pressures on their time. This often means they have less opportunity to focus and reflect on an experience in any detail. Whenever we can, we need to offer them the time to do so.

So what else can we do to encourage perseverance in children? Here are seven consistent actions worth considering:

◊ Point out some behavioural models around them, such as the classmate in a wheelchair who persists with a task, or a friend who patiently masters a new skill, or other family members who are tenacious in different aspects of their lives. Tell the stories over and over.

◊ Refer to movie characters who demonstrate perseverance. Many children's movies focus strongly on this theme. Think of examples such as *The Karate Kid*, which shows how relentless practice eventually pays off.

◊ Find books and stories about perseverance that are age appropriate, such as *The Tortoise and the Hare* for pre-schoolers.

◊ Help them to set specific goals. When they first write them down, encourage them to start with 'I will ...', and include a completion date. Then celebrate each success.

◊ Brainstorm a metaphor that represents perseverance for each child. This may include an animal or insect that struggles daily to survive, or an explorer who fought against the odds, or a plant that can thrive in the middle of a desert.

◊ Connect anything they accomplish to the practice they put in. 'Congratulations,' you might say. 'This is because of all those times you kept practising.'

◊ Children need at least one highly trusted adult who will support them through the difficult times when they want to give in. This may be a parent, a teacher, a coach or another reliable person who wants to see the best possible outcomes for the child.

Like everything else in life, there needs to be some balance here. Believe it or not, too much perseverance may not be good for you, just as a chocolate overdose can make you sick. One important life skill is to know when to concede gracefully and to accept that there is no point in continuing a project that is not working. If a child persists beyond all possible hope of accomplishing something, this may be an indication of obsessive-compulsive behaviour.

> The Slow philosophy does not mean we work at a snail's pace. It means we do everything at the *right* speed.

When distress is the only outcome of this fixation, they may come to resent ever starting the project. Card players talk about a time to hold and a time to fold. Drawing an incomplete project to a close is not necessarily a sign of weakness. It may be a sign of an agile thinker who understands how to find some balance between accomplishment and peace of mind. So how do we help them to find that fabled balance?

SUPPORTING THEIR PEACEFUL SOUL

In response to the daily scramble of modern life, the 'Slow movement' has grown steadily over the past few decades. In his book *In Praise of Slow*,[16, 17] Carl Honoré explains that the Slow philosophy does not mean we work at a snail's pace; it means we do everything at the *right* speed. In his words, it is about 'doing everything as well as possible, instead of as fast as possible. It's about quality over quantity in everything from work to food to parenting'. I believe that we

TALKING WITH THE NEXT GENERATION

WHEN THEY SAY

'I don't like all of these endless changes going on around me. Nothing feels comfortable anymore.'

SOME RESPONSES YOU MIGHT OFFER

'Yes, there is certainly a lot of change happening all the time. It is possible to feel overwhelmed by it all. Instead, **turn your thinking around and see change as an opportunity, rather than a threat.** Many changes will give you the chance to do amazing things with your life.'

'When lots of things are changing all around you, it challenges you to get rid of the time-wasting "extras" in your life. The "extras" are the things that take up too much of your time, and take lots of hard work, without giving you much benefit. Getting rid of those "extras" gives you more time to enjoy the experiences that are worthwhile for you.'

'We all feel overwhelmed some of the time, and want to run away from it all. Here's an alternative. **Deal with the issue by becoming more mindful.** This means learning how to be more at peace with your own thinking, in spite of everything rushing at you all at once. The secret is to focus on deep breathing. In 2, 3, 4, Hold 2, 3, 4, Out 2, 3, 4.'

need both Slow schools and Slow parenting, where the focus is placed on a smaller number of enriching experiences, rather than on doing as many things as possible.

Let's start by reconsidering the pace and pressure that is placed on senior school students. This pressure can lead to unsettling mental health issues that threaten their personal future. The World Health Organization reports that around 20 per cent of children and adolescents worldwide have mental disorders or problems.[18] Many factors contribute to this, although it doesn't help when adults give teenagers the impression that their final exams will determine the rest of their life. This is not true, although the prospect adds an overwhelming weight to a young person's mind.

Hard-nosed adults sometimes argue that this is how life works. It's tough, they say, but you must either sink or swim. Such an argument is vacuous, and does not deserve acknowledgement in a world that cares about its kids. It's our job, not to drown them in the deep end, but to teach them how to swim. In this case, the lesson would focus in part on finding some peace in their life.

So how do parents support their child's peaceful soul? Just love them. That's pretty well it. Oh, there are thousands of other things you can do to nurture a child's wellbeing and mental health. For now, rest assured that unconditional love is what matters most.[19] It gives children a foundation of peace and stability in their lives. Unconditional means that no conditions are placed on the act of love, without exception. Is it possible to practise this unconditional love and still challenge children to work hard? Of course it is. They are not mutually exclusive. In a climate of respect and open support, there is a better chance of encouraging children with their commitments.

Most parents around the world want their children to work hard. Some set very high expectations for their children. 'Tiger Mums' invite accusations of 'hothousing' in their attempts to fast-track their children's development. Is this hothousing a good thing? It depends on the child. If an overload of activities makes children uncomfortable or disillusioned, then it's worth rethinking the number of experiences you organise for them. If they cannot keep up, it doesn't necessarily mean they are lazy. It may mean their growing brain simply needs more time to process those experiences.

> Just because you rush around in your adult life does not mean children need to do the same at age seven.

Conversely, if they love the experiences and keep asking for more, then the broad range of activities is probably beneficial for them. Is it still possible to overload them? Probably. According to one British report, on average children in the UK are working on school and extracurricular activities for 46 hours a week, which is nine hours longer on average than their parents work.[20]

Most of those Tiger Mums may not agree with me, although there is merit in asking: Why does every minute need to be crammed with activity? Just because you rush around in your adult life does not mean children need to do the same at age seven. Every minute of their day does not have to be timetabled. Boredom isn't necessarily a bad thing. When children are bored, it's a great opportunity for them to create their own experiences, or even sometimes just to sit and daydream for a while. Inventors and scientists swear by it, so get children started early.

Although an imprecise science, mindfulness training is critical. Mindful children are fully focused on their everyday lives, while still experiencing their life in a peaceful state. Meditation practice is one way to steadily achieve this mode, but that takes valuable time. Given their busy lives, is it really worth their investing this amount of effort in meditating?

Research by the US-based Edutopia indicates that it is.[21] High-school students who practised daily focused meditation committed 50 per cent fewer rule infractions; they also accounted for 25 per cent fewer class absences and 35 per cent fewer suspension days. Daily meditation by students in Grades 1 to 7 led to significantly improved scores on validated attention-skills tests. Any other intervention that even vaguely approached these rates of improvement would be implemented without fail in every school and home. So how do we go about doing this?

Begin with the breath. Breathing is the basis for any form of mindful practice for children. Before they start an activity, show them how to breathe, such as 'In 2, 3, 4, Hold 2, 3, 4, Out 2, 3, 4'. For just a few minutes, play some relaxing music to create a peaceful mood for this breathing meditation. Pachelbel's Canon in B Minor works a treat, partly because it is in 4:4 time, which helps children to synchronise their breathing with the music.

Do your child's teacher a favour, and encourage children to practise this meditation for just a few minutes before heading off to school each morning. Fast-paced and violent video games, let alone the exhausting rush in the post-breakfast period, are not the best start for a focused day of learning. Imagine millions of families travelling to school and work each day with some meditative music floating through the car or their earbuds.

A morning meditation takes only a few minutes, so what about the rest of the day? Welcome to the concept of metacognition, which is all about developing your awareness of your own thoughts and feelings. Encourage them to stand back and observe themselves from a distance. Building on the self-talk described earlier, they might ask themselves two questions while they are observing themselves: What am I doing well? How might I do this differently?

Focus on what creates a sense of peace and certainty in their lives. One different way of looking at rapid change is to compile a list of things that are absolutely guaranteed not to change in their future. The list might include their love of their family, of playing sport, of their favourite music, of spending time with good friends. Sometimes the world seems to be changing too dramatically and we wonder: What else will change? At the same time, we need to ask: What will stay the same? Here's one special concept that is unlikely to change. We will continue to empathise with each other. In chapter 5, we'll explore why this capability is so important to our children's future lives.

CHAPTER 5

Heart-to-heart: enhancing empathy

WHAT IT'S ABOUT

Empathy is the key 21st century capability to balance the artificiality of the robot world. This chapter explores why empathy is so important and offers a practical range of ideas for developing this special capability in children. We begin by exploring why the world may become even more empathic this century.

#empathy #futureofempathy #worthofempathy
#techempathy #empathiclistening

THE PROMISE OF AN EMPATHIC FUTURE

The Human Library[1] loans out people for you to read. It is a non-profit organisation that allows users to 'borrow' a person instead of a book, and to be challenged on your belief systems through conversation with your loaned person. First developed in Copenhagen at the Roskilde Festival in 2000, Human Library events have taken place in over 70 countries around the world. Australia was the first country to establish a permanent library.

A mandatory requirement is that all borrowers be tolerant of diversity, given that difficult questions can be asked and authentic answers will be provided. The person on loan to you may be homeless or gay or Muslim or sexually abused or unemployed or many other variations on being 'different'. Empathy for others is the basic principle behind the Human Library, as it must be for the future of human relationships on this planet.

Although it is a difficult concept to measure, there are strong indications that human beings are becoming more competent at empathising with others. Earlier civilisations often displayed marked indifference or hostility to outsiders. Tribal warfare in medieval Europe was, in relative terms, nine times as deadly as any 20th century warfare or genocide.[2] If you prefer nonviolent interaction—and hopefully that applies to the vast majority of us—then you would much prefer to be alive today than at any other time in human history.

> It's an optimistic start to the 21st century for our children.

Since 1945, the world has entered a period known as the Long Peace, in which we have managed to avoid worldwide international bloodshed. While violent events are still taking place around the planet today, they directly affect a much smaller proportion of the world's population than in pre-18th century conflicts. Does this make today's violence acceptable? No, it doesn't. Can we assume that the current global trends will continue? There is no guarantee of that either. However, it's an optimistic start to the 21st century for our children.

In *The Better Angels of Our Nature*,[3] Steven Pinker explores what he claims to be a relative decline in violence throughout human history. According to him, there are many complex reasons for this progress. Rather than these improvements being attributed to biological or cognitive changes in humans, they can more likely be attributed to forces that influence our cultural and social patterns.

Cosmopolitanism is one of these historical forces. This includes the mass media, global literacy and international mobility that influence our cultural perspectives of other people and encourage us to relate to them in times of distress. Pinker outlines various trends of violence that are in decline, including what he calls 'the humanitarian revolution'. The 17th and 18th centuries marked a turning point in the use of judicial torture, slavery, sadistic punishments and even superstitious killings.

Referring to them as 'better angels', Pinker examines four motives that have led us away from violence and towards altruism and cooperation. One of these motives is empathy, which is the ability to understand and identify with the feelings of another person. This 'better angel' has every chance of continuing to fly. One reason for optimism is the upsurge in what is referred to as 'citizen journalism'—news and information disseminated by members of the public. Today anyone with a mobile phone can capture evidence of a human rights abuse and post it online.

At the international level, the Arab Spring is a powerful example of how this approach is influencing the world. Since 2010, online activists in the Middle East and North Africa have contributed to the pressure being placed on human rights violators. Citizen journalism is being driven by millions of people worldwide who care enough about a particular injustice to become more involved in challenging it.

Does our increasingly transparent society mean our children will live in a more empathic world, one filled with compassion and tolerance? While the 'better angel' of empathy may be on the rise in the long term, not all young people feel the spirit. Many who spend too much time online have developed a low boredom threshold and will simply turn something—or someone—off as soon as their interest flags. Voice-controlled virtual assistants such as Microsoft's Cortana and Amazon's Alexa can be treated with a complete lack of empathy, and there are no social consequences.[4] Perhaps these devices need to be programmed to respond to a child's request only when they hear a 'please'.

In the Western world, children live in smaller families than a century ago, with fewer opportunities for developing empathy with their siblings. Some studies[5] suggest that young people today are more concerned about their own interests than they are about the welfare of others. This does not necessarily mean that empathy is on the decline, however. In fact, 'Caring for others' is the second most frequently ticked box in many of these surveys. Most teenagers are understandably concerned about their future options, which is why a topic such as 'Worried about a job' is often their top selection.

So how will empathy rank in the future? This is not something we can easily predict. Rather, it is something we must *create*. At the risk of overworking a well-worn cliché, the world is fashioned from the billions of everyday actions taken by every one of us.

As a parent, what sort of world do you hope to see for your children? If you want a more empathic planet, then start with your own family. Encourage your children to become more aware of the people around them. Help them to appreciate that every unknown child they pass in the street, or meet online, has a life as full of joys and trials as their own. Teach them the value of being more empathic with everyone around them.

THE VALUE OF EMPATHY

One of my humble claims to fame is that I know Apple's Siri—the real Siri. Actually, there are several Siris around the world, and one of them is a magic lady called Karen Jacobsen. Born in Australia, Karen now lives in New York, and is an accomplished singer and professional speaker. She's also a great friend. A couple of years ago, I received a phone call from Karen, who had heard that I was going through a difficult time in my life.

From the other side of the world, she spent quite some time asking me lots of questions and checking on how I was coping. I was truly grateful for the empathy she displayed at the time. Later I had to laugh when the thought came to me: Siri had asked *me* lots of questions, rather than the other way around.

Imagine if every person on the planet one day in the future shows the same kind of empathy. You might say it is impossible, that some human beings will always display little or no empathy. I agree. But let's speculate on the possibilities for a few blissful moments. Every person you meet is interested in your welfare. Drivers respect all other drivers on the road. Disagreements are more easily resolved, because each side is sensitive to the other's needs and beliefs. Politicians pursue consensus, rather than relying on argument and vitriol. Obviously, humanity is too complicated for everyone to be this empathic. Or is it?

Perhaps everyone needs to become aware of the life-changing benefits of being a more empathic person. Empathy builds trust and a more positive connection between people. Making an effort to relate more closely to others improves our relationships. People may even like us more when we are authentically empathic.

> Empathy builds trust and a more positive connection between people.

Empathy is generally good for our emotional health, with one exception: we experience empathic distress when we become so involved in another person's emotional state that it compromises our own. Good counsellors know how to be empathic without taking upon themselves the distress being shared with them.

Empathy can help us to buy better gifts for others, because we make an effort to understand what the recipient would like. One study in Finland suggests that children learn more effectively when they have an empathic teacher.[6] The safe and supportive relationship established by a caring educator reinforces children's positive image of themselves.

TALKING WITH THE NEXT GENERATION

WHEN THEY SAY

'Being empathic with other people makes me uncomfortable. Why do I have to do it?'

SOME RESPONSES YOU MIGHT OFFER

'**There are lots of benefits to being empathic.** People will often like you more (although this is not the reason you do it). It helps you to understand other people better. It can lead to fewer misunderstandings and arguments with others, and it can even help you to be happier more of the time.'

'**When you are an adult, empathy will become more important than ever.** Many new jobs will need high empathy. The world is becoming increasingly diverse, which means that we need to develop a greater awareness of the different lives people live.'

'Remember that it doesn't make you a weak person to really care about other people. **It makes you a stronger person when you empathise.** Some people seem to think that empathy is a solely female characteristic. That's not correct. It's a human characteristic to relate to other people's needs and feelings, regardless of your gender.'

We sometimes explain empathy as 'walking a mile in someone else's shoes'. Back in 1933, George Orwell did just this before writing his first novel, the autobiographical *Down and Out in Paris and London*, which described poor and marginalised groups in those two cities at the time.[7] As part of his research, he worked as a dishwasher in hotel and restaurant kitchens in Paris and lived among tramps in east London. The insights he developed from these experiences led to his empathic portrait of the poor and disenfranchised of that time.

John Howard Griffin engaged in a similar project in 1959. A white man, he shaved his head, dyed his skin black and travelled around several southern US states.[8] He wrote about his unsettling experiences in *Black Like Me,* which fed into the growing civil rights movement of the time. There is great merit in children walking in someone else's shoes, at least in their imagination.

When children practise empathy, it can change their lives, as well as the lives of those they empathise with. Highly empathic children are less likely to engage in bullying, and more likely to stand up to those who do. Children who demonstrate sympathy and concern for others are more likely to develop sustainable friendships.

As young people approach working age, they will find that empathy is highly prized in many professions. Medical practitioners, social service workers, teachers and salespeople fall squarely into this category. These are also professions currently experiencing employment growth. Empathy can be taught at an early age, and the consequences can be life-changing.

HELPING CHILDREN TO PRACTISE EMPATHY

It's not often that a baby becomes the teacher for a class of children. In Roots of Empathy[9] it does just that. This program has been implemented in 10 countries around the world. It involves a local neighbourhood parent and baby visiting the same classroom once every three weeks for a full year.

The program instructor focuses on the baby in order to help the children identify their own feelings and the feelings of others. Babies bring out the empathic best in people of all ages. Programs such as Roots of Empathy offer sustainable, long-term benefits.

So what does it really mean for children to be empathic in their daily life with everyone, and not just babies? It means they can appreciate the other person's perspective. They feel compassion, listen deeply, and respond in a way that indicates they understand the other's words and feelings. Daniel Goleman[10] identifies three types of empathy:

1. *Cognitive empathy.* They know what the other person is feeling, and perhaps even what they are thinking. It does not mean they care, though. They are simply able to understand the other person's perspective.

2. *Emotional empathy.* They perceive what the other person is feeling, and they really care about them.

3. *Compassionate empathy.* Utilising the first two types of empathy, they then take action and provide practical support.

Think of these three types as the mind, the heart and the soul of empathy.

Harvard researchers have mapped out some child-rearing strategies for raising kind kids who care about others.[11] One idea is to give them frequent opportunities to be empathic. They might, for example, offer a hug to a younger sister who is feeling sad. The researchers point out that children need to learn two important empathic skills. One is to 'zoom in' and deeply listen to someone. The second is to 'zoom out' and learn how to see the bigger picture on what is occurring.

It is critical that you yourself model empathy. It is not just something you tell children to do. The most obvious modelling is your empathic support for your own family. Children also observe what you do when a shopkeeper serves you or when you walk past a homeless person on the street. For the children in your care, you are always on empathic show. Live up to your advice to them.

For empathy to become embedded in children's psyche, it needs constant practice and reflection. Have a regular conversation about the way they empathised with someone that day.

> Encourage them to become a little kinder than they need to be.

Ask them to explain what they did and how they felt while they were engaging with that person. Talk about what they might do tomorrow. Encourage them to become a little kinder than they need to be.

The family Facebook page usually indicates to other relatives and friends how serious we are about empathy. What is the general flavour of what you write in social media about the children? It's great to acknowledge the funny episode with the pet cat, or their successes in sport and academia. Equally important is to focus on social settings and empathy offered to others.

One outdated myth is that girls are better at empathy than boys. While there are indications that testosterone may partly inhibit an empathic response, empathy is a learned rather than a biologically determined behaviour.[12] Some boys—even grown-up boys—occasionally see empathy as a weakness of character. It may be time for them to move into the 21st century.

Children who have the confidence and capability to care about other people demonstrate strength of character. Empathy indicates inner strength. Such children have an internal core of resilience that enables them to more readily look outside themselves to others' needs and feelings.

Talk with them about the outmoded belief that 'nice' people finish last. In reality, nice people who balance their own needs with those of others will often finish first. The old belief was partly based on one-off experiments in which participants sought an immediate advantage, without needing to consider whether they would ever have to work with that person over the long term. Real life requires a consideration of long-term relationships.

Empathy is about to assume a global context for our children. In earlier times, we would demonstrate our care and concern for others in everyday situations at home, school and work. As we move towards the mid 21st century, children will have the opportunity to demonstrate empathy in an online world by using futuristic technology tools. The ability to offer immediate support to anyone anywhere will create a vast new landscape of care around the planet.

EMPATHY SUPPORTED BY HIGH TECH

Here's an example. *Be My Eyes*[13] helps visually impaired people to see. This ingenious free app connects two groups of people who may be anywhere in the world: visually impaired people who need someone to read something to them; and volunteers who can view a live video stream and read it out to the blind person. It might be as simple as the text on a street sign or the expiration date on a carton of milk.

One of life's basic tenets is that our many small efforts determine the collective quality of society, and our online world now gives us many opportunities to make these efforts. Whether it be empathising with a troubled friend for five minutes on Skype or helping a blind person to read a milk carton, these compassionate efforts use high tech to offer support to others.

Social media can help you become an amateur psychoanalyst to support your friends. One AI program can detect a person's possible depression with 70 per cent accuracy just by scanning the Instagram images this person shares on their site.[14] Even physicians can only manage 42 per cent. How does the program do this analysis? There is often a link between depression and reduced social activity. Also, photos posted by people who have been diagnosed with depression tend to be greyer, bluer and darker.

There are some indications that social media itself may contribute to their malaise, given that everyone except them seems to be having a wonderful life. This needs to be balanced by the social value of staying in contact with one's friends through the online world. Social media is another of the beautiful messes in the world today.

In real-life situations, specific software can accurately track your emotional state. Face recognition technology can interpret the 3000 micro-expressions that pass across your face at different times, and determine not just your mood but also what you are thinking, to some extent at least.[15] EQ-Radio can interpret your feelings by tracking your heart rate when wifi signals are bounced off your body.[16]

A future version of Snapchat Spectacles[17] may feature embedded facial recognition software that can detect your face, cross-reference that recognition with your social media feeds and flash the wearer a brief visual overview that includes your name, professional work and personal beliefs on different issues. If you have ever struggled with remembering names, you are going to love this technology. Just imagine approaching someone at a party, already knowing their attitudes to different issues.

As with every technology ever invented, these tools may be used for benefit or mischief. Is there an issue of privacy with Spectacles that can reveal so much about a stranger? Of

> Technologies such as these will enable us to help others much more easily.

course there is. It is very possible that a small percentage of the population will use the tools for unethical purposes, and mandatory safeguards will be necessary. On the optimistic side, technologies such as these will enable us to help others much more easily.

Analysing a friend's Instagram account might encourage you to offer much-needed support. A teacher could adjust a lesson, based on the emotional states of the children in the class. With your permission, a medical specialist or therapist might use these technologies to better understand your emotional state and provide more effective care.

Wearable devices may free up our time, allowing us to relate more closely with others. Future versions of Google Glass are likely to give workers hands-free and real-time access to vital information.[18] At present, doctors can spend more than one-third of their day grappling with electronic health data on their computer. If their advanced eyewear can perform such analysis instantly, they would have more time to support their patient directly.

Think of secondary school teachers who may work with more than 150 students every day. Imagine if they could move from child to child, instantly accessing all relevant data about that child's prior learning.

Will this software improve empathy between people? That will still depend on the personal capabilities of the professional involved, although having the necessary data is a great place to start.

Oral language is our core mode of communicating with other people. Perversely, one of the greatest impediments to global collaboration is that there are at least 6500 spoken languages around the world. More than 2.5 billion people speak only four of them, namely Mandarin, Spanish, English and Hindi. Just imagine if we were all able to talk with each other, and what a difference that would make to understanding and empathising across cultures. Now we can.

Google's translation service has come close to matching human translators[19], while Skype Translator[20] can help you to connect in eight different languages during voice calls and more than 50 languages if you are using instant messaging. The Earbud[21] is the world's first smart earpiece for translating between speakers using different languages. Although present versions require both the speaker and the listener to be wearing the device, later versions will translate from any spoken source.

Many of our devices will 'empathise' with us in an artificial way, depending on their programming. In the field of robotherapy,[22] a small robot will teach an autistic child some basic social skills, or a robotic system will guide stroke victims through their recovery exercises. These supportive robots may help someone to quit smoking. They may offer companionship in an aged care home. Socially assistive robots, as they are also called, may provide physical, social or cognitive support to infants, young adults or geriatrics.

Until now, one-on-one technological support has been offered through on-screen video or voice recordings. However, robots often stimulate better learning of skills or knowledge. While the person being assisted can too easily ignore support being given through a video on a screen, they are more likely to respond to a robot that is physically present with them. One intriguing turning point will come when children are able to design and 3D print their own robot for their personalised support.[23] And depending only on the designer's own creativity, it might have three ears, tell great jokes and be prepared to do their assignments for them.

EMPATHY AND THE ART OF LISTENING

There are not too many people on the planet with three ears, although most of us have two. We also have one mouth, and that 2:1 ratio probably indicates how much each needs to be used when we are talking with someone. Unfortunately, it is sometimes the other way around. Listening has gone a little out of fashion, and that may need to change.

The focus in TV sit-coms is too often on the ego-driven central character who delivers rapid-fire retorts laced with derogatory humour. Very rarely is the hero a quiet soul who listens respectfully to what others are saying. It just doesn't fit with the fast-paced, mischievous nature of such shows. The world would do well to focus on more heroes who really listen.

When you pay attention deeply and respectfully, you demonstrate an increased empathic connection with the speaker. The quality of your family life will be influenced by how well everyone listens to one another. Similarly, the quality of the workplace can be gauged by the degree to which people listen empathically, rather than seeking to impress through speaking. We are more likely to resolve issues if we make the effort to listen.

The Danish education system has recognised the impact of respectful listening. Every class engages in a one-hour session each week on empathy building, in which the children listen and respond to class members who want to resolve a problem. This Klassens Tid, or class time,[24] is a part of the national curriculum. The goal is to create a safe and cosy atmosphere, which the Danes call *hygge*.

They must be doing something correctly, given that Denmark ranked at number one in the World Happiness Report in 2016.[25] Other school classrooms around the world use variations on this dialogue approach.

What can we all learn from this? Engage in dialogue, listen respectfully and resolve problems whenever we can. Set up a similar process for the family, with a clear focus on resolving whatever issue any family member raises.

> As a parent, you will not only need to explain the listening standards; you will need to model them directly.

To do this, everyone involved listens deeply. As a parent, you will not only need to explain the listening standards; you will need to model them directly. Five levels of listening have been recognised.[26] At the first level you ignore the person speaking; you simply don't listen at all. At the second level you pretend to listen, but you won't remember much of what was said, because your attention was elsewhere. At the third level you listen selectively, paying attention to what interests you while ignoring anything else.

The fourth level is known as attentive listening. You listen carefully, although you're mainly thinking about how you will respond at some point. At the fifth level, empathic listening, you show profound respect for the speaker and listen with the sole intention of empathising. Listening is a key social skill for generating empathy.

We often hear about the difficulties of ever finding consensus in the Palestine/Israel conflict. However, very few media reports focus on initiatives that have been implemented to resolve the impasse in local communities. These successful projects focus on listening to the other side.

At the Hummus Bar, a small café in Kfar Vitkin, in central Israel, all customers are offered a 50 per cent discount on the food, with just one stipulation: that Arabs and Jews sit and eat together at the same table.[27] The main meal is stewed chickpeas and msabaha. One headline referred to the café's initiative as Chickpeace.

Another project also focuses on dialogue, although on a larger, more organised scale. The Parents Circle — Families Forum (PCFF) is a joint Palestinian and Israeli initiative.[28] It involves more than 600 families, all of whom have lost a close family member in the prolonged conflict. Reconciliation is sought through open dialogue in public meetings and education forums and through the media. The participants have found that when they listen, they learn and achieve more.

Few of the world's complex problems are ever fixed by force. Resolution needs to be based on empathic dialogue in an everyday 'human library'. Our children will lead a life worth living when they acknowledge their differences and support those who need help. Let's start with our own families and schools, and teach our children one of the most important capabilities for the future — the 'better angel' of empathy.

CHAPTER 6

We live and learn: embedding a love of inquiry

WHAT IT'S ABOUT

The Next Generation will learn throughout their lifetime. Constant updating of skills and knowledge will be critical. Children today who love to inquire will be well placed in this learning future. Let's start with an example of a particular child who loved to learn.

#inquiry #passionforlearning #wow #aha
#personalisedlearning #globallearningcommons
#neweducation

A PASSION FOR LEARNING

He was only seven years old when he received the most exciting birthday present of his life. It was a huge hardcover book that featured many of the world's most fascinating animals. His parents were certainly not wealthy, and it must have stretched their budget to purchase such a luxury item. The glossy pages were filled with wondrous images, and the descriptions stirred his brain with the joy of discovery.

The young boy revisited that massive book hundreds of times, poring over every word and photo. This single book bewitched him, and inspired him to continue reading and learning all his life. I know all about that little boy, because he was me. And I can still remember the joy I felt with the turning of every page.

Two special words kept bursting out as I lived in that book: 'Aha!' and 'Wow!' We need to encourage these responses in every child's life. *Aha* expresses their delight and surprise when they 'get' something for the very first time. Ask children to exclaim 'Aha!' whenever they suddenly understand something properly for the first time. It beats playing 'I Spy' in the back of the car.

When might you say 'Wow'? If you have ever seen a giant glacier, or fireflies in a dark cave, or a double rainbow, or the Northern Lights, or anything else that fills you with a sense of awe, then you probably said 'Wow!' Recently, I read that astronomers have revised their calculations on the number of galaxies in the universe,[1] and it sure got me thinking. They used to maintain there were up to 200 billion. 200 billion! Not 200 000, which would be a big enough number, or even 200 million, but 200 *billion*. That's '2' with 11 zeros after it.

Remember that our entire Milky Way, which itself contains between 100 and 400 billion stars, is just one of those 200 billion galaxies in the observable universe. However, it has recently been determined that there are 10 times more galaxies than previously thought. Astronomers have now estimated that there are up to two *trillion* galaxies out there. Wow!

A household or classroom where *ahas* and *wows* are part of the everyday discourse is a superb environment for stimulating children's learning. These words can provoke them into observing the world around them, imagining everything around them as a learning opportunity.

Author Neil Pasricha certainly knows how to do this. He once spent nearly three years writing a daily blog called '1000 Awesome Things',[2] posting one delightful life experience each day. Number 758 was celebrating your pet's birthday, even though it has no idea what's going on. Setting a new high score on a video game was #602, while #117 involved driving down an old road between rows of trees that reach over and touch each other to form a canopy overhead.

I once heard of a New Zealand teacher who compiled a list of 100 awesome things about being a 10-year-old with her class each year. This recognition of awesomeness would be an enticing

> What are the 100 most awesome things about us as a family?

challenge for everyone at the dinner table each night. Imagine asking: What's the most awesome thing that one of us—or each of us—discovered today? Over time you might even ask: What are the 100 most awesome things about us as a family?

If you're hoping that children will grow up to be inspiring and engaging human beings who think that life and learning are awesome, then live it yourself. As much as it initially feels easier to hand this responsibility off to other teachers or coaches, the reality is that parents are the first teacher when it comes to enthusing children about life.

Do whatever you can to amass more *ahas* and *wows* rather than regrets in your own life. Once you lose interest in doing this, you may even become boring, which means you won't be the best role model. Your children may look at you and think, *Is that what it's like to be a grown-up? I'm not sure I want to go there!*

HOW CHILDREN CAN BECOME EFFECTIVE LEARNERS UP AHEAD

Now to put all those *ahas* and *wows* into everyday practice. Regularly learning something new is critical for the brain. The 'use it or lose it' adage applies to all ages. Here are three exciting ways of engaging children in learning that boosts their brain:

◊ Get them enthused about reading. In a perfect world, every parent will have read 1000 books to their child by the age of five. That's one book a day for nearly three years. Consider it a priceless investment in your child's future learning.

◊ Encourage them to learn another language. Given that 80 per cent of the world's population does not speak English, there is merit in becoming multilingual in a global economy. Children who study a language at elementary level score higher on tests in reading, language arts and maths.[3]

◊ Support children in learning a musical instrument. It improves brain functioning, and can raise their IQ by seven or more points.[4]

Children's learning can now be undertaken even more successfully than in the past. The recent research on pedagogy—the art and science of learning for 4- to 18-year-olds—has clarified many key elements that enhance a child's education. Those elements include deep understanding, higher order thinking, self-regulation and narrative. Applying these approaches doesn't mean that the basic skills are neglected. Rather, they are now learned and consolidated in richer and more effective ways.

Fabled educator Joan Dalton explains:'In a world where information is growing exponentially, the meaning of "knowing" has shifted from being able to consume, remember and reproduce information to one where learners actively construct understanding to create knowledge that is new and usable to them'.[5]

We all want children to get excited about learning. It is a natural progression to develop deeper understandings through challenging and enticing learning experiences. This understanding is more likely to occur when children see meaning and relevance in what they are learning, and when they continually make new connections to what they already know. How can we help them to do this?

Give children the opportunity to apply their new-found knowledge in practical ways. It gives their learning a purpose and will also show whether they have understood what they learned. Explore the difficult questions, rather than just the basic information. Study extinction rather than dinosaurs. Research greed rather than money. Ask *why* and *how*, and not simply *what*. Remind kids everywhere that this more complex learning is not always meant to be fun. Too much is made of learning needing to be 'fun'. On the contrary, this more complex thinking can be exasperating and outright difficult.

In other parts of this book, I have described some amazing technologies that may save us from needing to learn new skills. As an example, translation devices already help us to understand a different language being spoken to us. Does this mean we won't need to learn most new things? Not necessarily. While the technology may make life easier in some ways, our beautiful brains still need to be exercised.

The 10 000-hour rule is often mentioned in relation to learning a new skill. Merely practise something for that number of hours, according to this theory, and you will master the skill. This is not always true. It depends on the type of practice you do in that time.[6] Mindless, unfocused drill repetitions are less likely to work and basically waste your time. Practice is more effective when it is taken seriously.

> You don't just want your children to learn. You want them to *want* to learn.

Encourage children to regulate their own learning. You don't just want them to learn. You want them to *want* to learn. How can you help with this? Start by thinking about who is asking the most questions.

You or them? While you might wish to test their knowledge initially, richer understanding is more likely to develop when they know how to ask worthwhile questions themselves. This gives them a sense of ownership over their learning.

Insightful questions are even more important than the answers, because they help children to discover many more answers by themselves. One practical way of building up this skill is to play some question games in which the child talks about an issue — such as their latest Minecraft update — while you continually intervene with questions, such as 'How do you know that?' or 'Can you give an example of that?' or 'Why do you believe that?' Then change places, with them asking you the questions while you explain what you know.

Inquiry is a critical capability for the mid 21st century. It means children want to find out about something, and ask great questions to explore it further. Questions drive inquiry. No matter what changes lie ahead, an inquiring mind has a better chance of making sense of it all.

There is magic in a child knowing how to work through a full inquiry process as they learn about a new topic. I know of one 10-year-old who wanted to find out whether it was possible for humans to live on Mars. While there are many variations on the structure of a learning inquiry, she worked through this process:

1. What exactly do I want to find out?

2. What do I already know about this?

3. What are my initial questions?

4. What learning steps will I take to find answers to those questions?

5. Given my learning up to now, what further questions do I want to ask?

6. What will I do with what I find out?

TALKING WITH
THE NEXT GENERATION

WHEN THEY SAY

'I'm bored with learning new things all of the time.'

SOME RESPONSES YOU MIGHT OFFER

'From the moment you were born, you were designed to be a learner. **If you don't keep learning, you end up staying the same all through your life.** This is not a good idea. If you're not careful, you may eventually become boring even to yourself, let alone to others around you. Instead, it's important to become more interesting by learning lots of new things.'

'**Not all learning is easy and fun.** Most of the time, you have to struggle when learning something new. Too many kids say their school learning is boring, although that's often because they have to work hard on what they're doing. The reality is that if you want to get better at something, you have to learn about it and practise a lot.'

'**If you are getting bored with your learning, then find some different ways of doing it.** Back in the 20th century, your grandparents could only go to a library or a classroom to find out about anything. Now you can learn anything just by being online. Look for some great news feeds or YouTube channels or websites that keep giving you plenty of amazing new ideas and information.'

Following these steps will help this 10-year-old to pinpoint her learning needs throughout her lifetime, and then to put them into practice. Imagine all of those adult learning experiences lying in wait for her: new work skills, relationship issues, personal interests she hopes to explore. Having her very own inquiry process will give her the confidence to see the learning as an opportunity rather than an imposition. And the inquiry questions that focus on *my* and *I* personalise her learning.

PERSONALISED LEARNING JUST FOR YOUR CHILD

Many professions now offer an individualised service approach to their clients. Personalised medicine[7] can pinpoint your symptoms at the molecular level and then recommend optimal therapies or drugs specifically for you. This targeted approach will even predict your risk for a particular disease. 3D printers can produce some of your prescribed medicines, printed according to your requirements.

We are moving closer to personalised learning in which we organise experiences to cater directly for each child's needs. Perhaps a child is struggling with quadratic equations but is highly competent in Shakespearean sonnets? We can cater for their strengths and weaknesses. This approach will make the 20th century version of one-size-fits-all education a distant memory.

Learning analytics software[8] can target the specific needs of a child, and a good educator can then recommend worthwhile interventions. It may involve specialised coursework that is online, video based and supported by continuous feedback from automated systems. This everyday micro-learning may involve individual study or working with a team of four other children who are engaged on the same project. Those four children may even live in different countries around the world. All of this personalised learning can then be organised into what is called a Learning Playlist.[9]

Think of the last time you arranged a music playlist. Perhaps it was for a party at your home. You probably thought about who was coming, then created a collection of songs you thought would appeal to them. A Learning Playlist works on the same principle. Sometimes with the advice of a teacher or parent, a child chooses their learning experiences for the next few weeks, arranging them on an electronic device if available. This ensures that the learning plan is always at their fingertips, along with access to all necessary videos and links. Ideally, by the time they turn 10 years old, children will be consistently refining their own Learning Playlist.

They start by choosing four or five learning experiences. These may be a combination of school projects and assessment tasks, personal outside interests and perhaps one provocative challenge that will really stretch their abilities. As one experience is completed, assessed and reflected on, another takes its place. The Learning Playlist is not a list of things they can already do. There would be little point in that, given that the purpose is to map out new learning.

Children need to be involved in choosing their Learning Playlist experiences. We want to reach the point where they are maintaining it by themselves. One reason some teenagers lose incentive with their learning is that it is done *at* them, and perhaps *for* them, while not as often *with* them. They need purpose to drive their learning. The best purpose arises from them wanting to learn it, and from making the choices themselves.

> One reason some teenagers lose incentive with their learning is that it is done *at* them, and perhaps *for* them, while not as often *with* them.

Personalised learning will also draw on technologies that offer individual support. Most young people love to interact with smart toys. Mattel's latest Hello Barbie[10] is a taste of the support mechanisms to come. Using voice recognition technology, this interactive doll can listen to a child's conversation, then provide a contextual comment from the 8000 different responses in its online memory bank.

In just a few years from now, similar devices (hopefully they won't look like Barbie) will be programmed to provide explicit daily support for every child. With face recognition technology also built into the device, it will determine whether they understand the work, and even partly the child's mood, and will adjust the learning experience accordingly. Might these devices replace teachers? Not for a long time, although they will certainly support what teachers do.

For parents, it will be like having a teacher at home who supports their children with their home study, which cannot come too soon for some. This technology-based personalised learning will transform the way we help them to learn, although it might sometimes come at a cost. For example, there are concerns about a child's privacy when they use Hello Barbie. All conversations are recorded in the Cloud, although legislation strongly protects how it can be used, and parents can delete anything they wish.

An online campaign at #hellnobarbie[11] protested against the sale of this doll, with claims that privacy and creativity were compromised. To give Mattel some credit, they made an effort to develop responsible answers for Hello Barbie. Here are two examples:

Child: 'I'm getting bullied in school.'

Hello Barbie: 'That sounds like something you should talk to a grown-up about.'

Child: 'Do you think I'm pretty?'

Hello Barbie: 'Of course you're pretty, but you know what else you are? You're smart, talented and funny.'

One-on-one devices similar to Hello Barbie will eventually deliver effective personalised learning for children, although many other online education support systems will continue to rely on a human instructor. One UK initiative is already pairing up teachers and students from different parts of the world. Third Space Learning[12] provides weekly maths support for nearly 4000 primary students, who are each matched up with a tutor in India or Sri Lanka for

45 minutes at a time. Artificial intelligence software monitors every one of these lessons, with the aim of improving both the child's learning performance and the tutor's instruction.

The whole world is becoming one vast classroom, with an endless array of learning materials available online for directly supporting each child. The *Encyclopaedia Britannica* is no longer a core resource for parents and teachers. They now have access to the global learning commons—the largest collation of learning resources the world has ever known. So what is a global learning commons? Depending on your age, you may even be asking: What is the *Encyclopaedia Britannica*?

THE DIGITAL WORLD AT THEIR FINGERTIPS

The *Encyclopaedia Britannica*[13] was first published in Edinburgh around 1768. It became the most comprehensive research tool for millions of people over the next two centuries. However, the online world rapidly surpassed this paper-based resource, and the 2010 version of 32 volumes and 32640 pages was the last printed edition. Today, a 10-year-old can borrow Mum's mobile phone, and access more information than was ever published in all of the earlier encyclopaedias put together.

Welcome to the global learning commons of the 21st century, in which a vast amount of the world's knowledge is available online, literally at the fingertips of every child. This open availability of knowledge has already challenged all schooling, training and higher education systems to comprehensively reframe how they operate. Learning is no longer just offered during set times in a physical location. Exhaustive information on every conceivable topic is available anytime and anywhere.

MOOCs[14] will play a growing part in this availability. When first introduced in 2008, Massive Open Online Courses promised to revolutionise the worldwide delivery of learning. Until recently they rarely did. The early versions involved little more than a camera positioned at the rear of a classroom, with the video recording placed online for others to watch.

They have come a long way since then, with some of today's versions rivalling the sophistication of the latest movie blockbuster. Many MOOCs have become an academic combination of Silicon Valley and Hollywood, which is one of the many criticisms directed at the phenomenon. Others see this entertainment focus as a saviour that will advance education for both young and old.

Some detractors draw attention to a course completion rate of only 10 per cent with many MOOCs. If this occurred in a secondary school, college or university, they argue, the course would be considered an abject failure. However, there are grey areas involved with these low completion rates.[15] While such statistics can sometimes indicate that attendees are just not interested in the course, many of those people may have simply wanted to experiment with a part of the course.

> Just In Time learning, rather than Just In Case learning, is sometimes more suitable for a rapidly changing world.

One benefit of a MOOC is that it delivers what you need when you need it. Just In Time learning, rather than Just In Case learning, is sometimes more suitable for a rapidly changing world. Alternative microcredit systems such as Mozilla Open Badges,[16] in which the student can verify their attainment of a competency from a short course, will become increasingly popular. Rapid updating of skills will be a vital requirement in a working future, and the flexible availability of these nanodegrees will suit our children's lifestyle.

The entertainment value of many online courses has obvious appeal for children. Their learning can benefit strongly from an informative and enticing MOOC.[17] The clamour from some aged education critics for a return to 'chalk and talk' is both nonsensical and embarrassing. Nearly every child under 18 in many countries has grown up on a cognitive diet of fast-paced action and immersive storylines. Surely their academic learning is allowed to be exciting too.

Some schools offer a process called the 'flipped classroom', in which children view the online videos at home for the initial background content, then the teacher provides intensive follow-up support for learning the course material when they are at school. If your school does not offer this opportunity, there are still endless choices that involve learning at home.

The Khan Academy[18] has developed a well-earned reputation for its video courses. They are provided free, although, like Wikipedia, they will occasionally ask for donations. Duolingo, one of the biggest language learning sites in the world, helps you to tap into the expertise of people who speak a different language. Coursera, EDX, Udemy and iTunes U are noteworthy for the quality of their offerings. Many reputable universities offer accredited MOOCs through these platforms.

YouTube Education and TED-Ed are free, and provide many entertaining short videos. YouTube is the ultimate 'how to' source on the planet, with some of the most helpful three-minute videos made by other children. There is no shortage of stimulating and relevant online material. The concern is that there is often too much choice. This is when the skill of searching online becomes a critical competency.

Get online with your children, then type the words 'How to search on Google'—into Google, of course. Spend just one hour together exploring the practical time-saving ideas you find, and encourage them to start building the suggestions into their searches from then on. This single hour may very likely save your children hundreds of hours of wasted searching for the rest of their school career. The benefit to your own work will be just as momentous.

There are many other search engines you can use as well. One of my favourites is DuckDuckGo,[19] partly for the name, and partly because they do not tag any of your online activity. If you love mathematics, and you want your children to enjoy it too, then the computational knowledge engine at WolframAlpha[20] will appeal. Enter an algebraic equation, for example, and it will outline all of the steps required to reach the solution.

The global learning commons changes how everyone can acquire an education. Only a few decades ago, we needed to go to school or university to source any new knowledge we required. Now we type in a brief search entry, or we just ask Siri to get us started. Our children are already directly involved in the greatest learning revolution in history. So what will draw all of this together? The key is to create education frameworks that prepare our children for the mid 21st century.

IMAGINING EDUCATION FOR THE FLEXIBLE FUTURE

The narrator of the 1884 satirical novel *Flatland*[21] is a square named A Square, who lives in a two-dimensional world. One fateful day the square meets a three-dimensional sphere (whose name is A Sphere!), and he struggles to comprehend how such a creature might exist. In the mid 21st century, the challenges to our children's thinking will be as disruptive as the 3D sphere was to the 2D square.

Some might think of today's schooling system as a square. It is full of great educators who care deeply about their students, and the vast majority of those educators work excessive hours. The dilemma is that they are working in a factory-based system designed for an earlier time. So what might we do to develop an enticing system that better represents the three-dimensional sphere?

> Imagine if every school structure on the planet disappeared overnight.

Let's play with an edgy conjecture here. Imagine if every school structure on the planet disappeared overnight. Children and teachers would arrive the next morning, and find a bare patch of dirt. Some children would celebrate, which in itself probably tells us something about the present system. Other than quelling the partying, what would society do to create a new 'education' for the mid 21st century?

Fast forward a couple of years, and think past the initial disruptions that would take place. There would be many. Given that we are so accustomed to children needing to attend a centralised physical space for learning, we would struggle to work out what to do with them. The cost of rebuilding would be prohibitive. The lack of resources would impede whatever temporary platforms were put in place.

The first step in planning this future learning framework would be to craft a new learning narrative. The 20th century story was that children must spend 12 or more years relentlessly learning material in subjects they sometimes didn't even like, then study further at a college or university, or do an apprenticeship. The new narrative would prepare children for a life filled with more flexible possibilities.

Here are some options for implementing this vibrant learning environment. Some of these proposals are already in place. Remember that this list is not one for adjusting the present education system. That would be a different list, at least in part. This one is for creating an entirely new learning platform from the beginning:

◊ Fewer new schools will be built. Instead, a more creative approach would consider the refurbishment of unused inner-city office buildings or deserted industrial complexes. A 'learning place' will become anywhere that has an internet connection or an accredited wise mentor.

◊ Small teams of teachers will coordinate learning experiences in a less regulated environment. This might mean a school, children's homes, parents' workplaces, or parks, museums or makerspace locations. Learning support may include a combination of online instruction and focused mentoring with individual children and their families.

◊ Any new learning places will be designed for better learning, rather than crowd control. Fresh, inviting environments will use natural lighting and creative design to improve children's focus on their learning.

◊ By the 2030s, more of those learning environments will be virtual, with children appearing in multiple locations around the world each day.

◊ Artificial intelligence assistants will be provided for each child. These assistants will competently develop the student's basic skills in a gamified online environment, which will release teachers for more advanced thinking tasks and emotional support for the children. The same AI system will constantly assess the child's learning and use the results to adjust the next study activities.

◊ Voice translation devices and telepresence capability will allow gifted teachers to work with anyone, anywhere on the planet. The skills and the personality of the best fit teacher will be matched with individual children according to specific needs.

◊ A Learning Playlist will become the basis for most of their learning. Education professionals will constantly fine-tune the playlist and negotiate with the child about the material listed. This negotiation will occur regularly online, with a consistent check-in at a physical location.

◊ Many playlist items will be real-life learning experiences that give context to the curriculum. These may range from an interactive website design for a local environmental action group, to an app that lets students know when their bus is due to arrive, to a how-to video about an aspect of playing Minecraft.

◊ Educators will work with other public services, reputable non-profit foundations, and small and large businesses to co-create a futuristic curriculum. This will prepare children for anything that may be up ahead, without exception. The curriculum will focus predominantly on enterprise capabilities such as critical and creative thinking, adaptive agility, solution-finding, digital literacies and interpersonal communication.

In this new education world, we will attract the most inspiring, intelligent and open-minded people on the planet to the teaching profession. At the same time, we will give explicit, unwavering support to those already there to become even more exceptional. Will all of these proposals cost a lot of money? Some may, although it would become even more expensive if quality learning were not implemented. Education is an investment, not a cost.

Let's come back to the present. Are all school buildings going to disappear overnight? I certainly hope not, although the dilemma is that we need some sort of drastic action to stimulate us into new ways of thinking about learning. If it's not the disappearance of the buildings, what else might have a similar effect? The delivery of advanced one-on-one learning through artificial intelligence is one possible incentive. A very different work-less and wealth-less world may be another.

The reality is we are already in the midst of these changes. It's time to respond to them.

Developing the capabilities of adaptive agility, empathy and inquiry outlined in these past three chapters is a critical first step. Now we come to the actions. Great learning paves the way for the implementation of what a child has learned and understood. In the third section of this book, we will reveal many exciting options for these actions. Let's begin, in chapter 7, with the development of enterprise.

PART III

ACTIONS FOR CREATING AN EXTRAORDINARY LIFE

CHAPTER 7

What's the big idea: stimulating their creative enterprise

WHAT IT'S ABOUT

The Next Generation are likely to become the most prolific entrepreneurs in human history. Many will want to control their own destiny, and offer their own contributions in their professional and personal life. This chapter is full of ideas for developing their enterprising spirit. Let's begin by exploring how the Next Generation will engage in entrepreneurship differently from earlier generations.

#initiative #entrepreneurship #humanenterprise #play
#creativegenius #youngentrepreneurs

GENERATING HUMAN ENTERPRISE

Youth is no barrier to entrepreneurial activity. Cassidy Goldstein was 11 years old when she invented the Crayon Holder.[1] It is sometimes the very simple things that can lead to productive results. When her crayon pieces broke or were too small to hold onto, she found a plastic tube used for keeping roses fresh. She slipped a crayon piece into the tube—and unwittingly invented her crayon holder. She filed a patent, and eventually received royalties from the sale of the product.

When people hear stories like this, they often make comments like, 'It's so obvious. Why didn't I think of that before?' or 'How did she work that out at her age?' People have always said that about new inventors, and they always will. They have even said it of the founders of some of the biggest corporations in history. Back in 2004, Mark Zuckerberg co-founded Facebook at the age of 19; Bill Gates created Microsoft in 1975 at age 23, and Steve Jobs started up Apple in 1976 when he was 21.

Younger people do enterprise differently. A 2016 Global Entrepreneur Report[2] found that whereas in the 20th century the baby boomer generation launched their first business at the average age of 35, millennials launch their first business at the average age of 27. The report, which surveyed 2600 entrepreneurs in 18 countries, found that younger people are starting businesses earlier and are much more positive than their older peers about making an increased profit in the next year.

The report also noted that these millennial entrepreneurs approach social contribution differently. Baby boomers often focused on the business first, considering their philanthropic offering later once they had become successful. Millennials consider their social impact and build it into their business at an early stage.[3]

Will all teenagers want to create an ingenious new Facebook or Apple, or even something as simple as crayon holders? While some may develop their own technology empire or new product, others will happily work as a salesperson or a nurse when they leave school. Enterprising people will not necessarily become the CEO of their own company. They may just as easily apply their enterprising flair to a career such as teaching.

We call them *intrapreneurs*. They are employees who engage in entrepreneurial activity while working full-time for an organisation. They still perform their regular work, they receive a wage and some holidays. At the same time, they generate a stream of fresh ideas for revolutionising their profession. Employers delight in finding bright young intrapreneurs who can think critically and creatively with a future focus.

How do young geniuses like this create and implement their ideas? They are usually highly intelligent,

Younger people do enterprise differently.

they are prepared to ask lots of questions and they often make use of what are called enterprise skills. These skills can include critical and creative thinking, digital literacy and financial literacy.

These enterprise skills are not just applicable to geniuses who have become billionaires by the age of 20. They are a special set of skills that can boost *any* young person's chances of successful employment. The beauty of enterprise skills is they are transferable between occupations, whereas technical on-the-job skills are more specific to each profession.

An innovative non-profit organisation called the Foundation for Young Australians (FYA) consistently champions improvements for teenage lives. In its 2016 'New Basics' report,[4] FYA pointed out that the demand for enterprise skills is increasing rapidly. Based on early career job ads in the previous three years, the requirement for digital literacy has increased by 212 per cent, critical thinking by 158 per cent and creativity by 65 per cent.

Wages also are higher for young job-seekers who have these enterprise skills, with a skill such as problem-solving paying $7745 more per year, and presentation skills $8853 more. So what can we do to further develop these enterprise skills?

To an extent we are already doing it. Welcome to enterprise education,[5] which has been implemented in schools around the world for many years. It is the education system's version of preparing children for life beyond school, and encompasses everything from community service projects to student-initiated businesses to giving students an authentic say in the organisation of the school through student councils.

One powerful approach is to offer classroom learning tasks that develop solutions to real-life issues. Most parents and teachers have been barraged by the perennial question 'Why do we have to do this?' from young people faced with an overload of study material. A part-solution is to provide some real-life purpose for the learning, such as being accountable to industry professionals who have collaborated with the children on a project. The most exciting part of all is when young entrepreneurs develop their own idea and put it into action.

YOUNG ENTREPRENEURS IN ACTION

A child's kerbside lemonade stall is very 20th century. Admittedly, if you saw one being operated by a 10-year-old today, you would still stop and buy their product. Children deserve to be supported, even if only for their initiative. More recently, some young people have moved far beyond lemonade sales. Now they develop ideas that benefit the whole world.

In 2015, 15-year-old Hannah Herbst won the Discovery Education 3M Young Scientist Challenge with a small floating probe that converts the natural movements of the ocean into usable electricity.[6] It cost her just $12 for a 3D-printed propeller, a small pulley, and a hydroelectric generator. The device will potentially provide cheap power to millions of people in developing countries.

When a young child loses an arm in an accident, the financial impact on the family can be significant. A single prosthetic arm may cost more than US$65 000, and will need to be continually replaced as their body grows. At least, that was the case until Easton LaChappelle[7] did some brilliant thinking. At the age of 16, he developed a 3D-printed prosthetic arm that can be controlled by the user's thinking … and it costs just $500.

First he made a robotic arm out of fishing wire, Lego and a 3D printer. After dismantling a computer game in which players control the movement of a ball by thought alone, he translated its mechanics into his robotic device. The result is a prosthetic arm that is controlled by the wearer's thinking. The files for his invention can be downloaded for free.

Is there merit in dropping out of school to pursue a dream? Fifteen-year-old Ben Pasternak[8] thought so when, in 2015, he developed the game Impossible Rush, which headed to the top of the Apple App Store charts. After securing funding from Silicon Valley investors, and being invited to the offices of Google and Facebook, he moved from Sydney to New York to develop further products. His latest effort is an app called Flogg, which lets Facebook users list, buy and sell their unwanted items. Mark Zuckerberg must be keeping a watchful eye on this young Aussie.

The practical implementation of enterprise is called entrepreneurialism. Perhaps your children will throw caution to the 21st century wind and test their resolve and ingenuity with a new business for the 2030s. If so, they might benefit from an after-hours entrepreneur club or short course that teaches them start-up skills ranging from website development to crowdfunding to simple financial planning strategies.

In Melbourne, Frankston High School offer an entrepreneur program to Year 9 and 10 students, who are required to contribute earned money to a social cause they care about.[9] St Paul's School in Brisbane run a 16-week after-school Entrepreneur's Club for 15 Year 7 to 12 students at a time. When they finish the course, they pitch their idea to potential investors. High Tech High school[10] in San Diego base much of their classroom learning on real-life enterprise projects.

Club Kidpreneur[11] conducts an annual entrepreneurial challenge in Australian schools. Primary school children develop a product for their business and sell it on Market Day. Their businesses have ranged from a lemonade stand to a parent advice service. They then donate all their profits to a social cause of their choice. The children upload a video pitch and the winners appear at high-profile events. Since 2010, more than 600 schools have been involved.

One factor influencing children's enterprise capability may be the size of the community in which they live. While they can still be highly enterprising in a small rural centre, there are some advantages to a large city. A larger population centre offers more resourcing and networking opportunities. In *Where Good Ideas Come From*,[12] Steven Johnson points out that a city that is 50 times bigger than a town will be 150 times more innovative.

Name a problem, and there is sure to be someone who is resolving it.

The number and proportion of people living in cities worldwide has changed dramatically over the past 200 years. In 1800, only 3 per cent of the world's population lived in urban areas; today, the figure is around 54 per cent. In 2050, it is projected to be about 70 per cent.[13] There are now over 400 cities with a population of more than one million people.

While massive cities sometimes have considerable drawbacks— one-seventh of the world's population live in urban slums—they also provide greater opportunities for networking and sharing. The increasing proportion of the world's population living in cities is one reason the world is on the cusp of an entrepreneurial revolution.

Fuelled by this ideas transformation, today's children will increasingly become solution-finders for the world's dilemmas. Don't expect them to sit back passively while there are issues to be resolved. Name a problem, and there is sure to be someone who is developing a solution. The number of batteries that end up in landfills each year is one such issue. In the United States alone that number is three billion, collectively weighing 180 000 tonnes.

Perhaps Vancouver's Ann Makosinski can help with her Hollow Flashlight.[14] At the age of 15, she developed a simple torch, powered by the warmth from your hand, that needs no batteries or solar charge. Just imagine if one of your children came up with a remarkable idea like that. Sound too fanciful? Someone will end up doing it. Why not your own children? If this initiative even slightly appeals to you, then get ready for a surprisingly simple strategy to generate their entrepreneurship at a young age. The solution? Just let them play.

LET THE CHILDREN PLAY

When children engage in play they develop skills that help them for a lifetime. If you don't believe this, then just ask Lego. The 30-year-old Lego Foundation, funded by a quarter of their after-tax profits, is dedicated to reimagining learning in educational settings.[15] In short, its focus is on redefining the importance of play in children's lives.

Now, Lego sell all of those colourful building blocks, so you would expect them to adopt this stance. At least they make the effort to invest in something important to children's lives. In 2016, they even set up a 'Lego professorship of play' at Cambridge University. Their funded research is adding to the body of worldwide studies that demonstrates convincingly that children need time to play.

Lego and many educators want to see children playing more, but some political leaders around the planet seem unconvinced. In a world obsessed with academic achievement, they are too often neglecting the power of play in young children's lives. Where did we go wrong with this? Unstructured play is critical for the cognitive and social development of young people.[16]

Here's a reality check. Think of those children when they are 25 years old, not just when they are five. To replace play with rigorous study is very short-term thinking. In the long term, children will achieve more highly in their academic work when they have been given the opportunity to play. We now know enough about child development to understand that spontaneous childhood play contributes positively to what is called executive functioning.

As we grow we develop a critical set of cognitive skills or functions to organise ourselves.[17] These skills include impulse control, which helps us to think before blurting out inappropriate comments, and task initiation, which relates to the ability to get started and take action with a task. Other executive functions include emotional control, working memory and self-monitoring. In *Focus: The Hidden Driver of Excellence*, Daniel Goleman explains, 'Teaching executive skills to preschoolers makes them more ready for their school years than does a high IQ or having already learned to read'.[18] While there are many strategies for steadily developing executive functions, one of the most vital is for children to engage in play.

Two different types of play are critical. The first is free play, which might include anything from creating a series of spontaneous drawings to constructing a tent out of blankets and chairs. Free play stimulates children to use their imagination. Trust the research, and allow your child to engage in this free play. The second is structured play: you might sign them up for a season with a sports team or a six-week creativity course.

How can my children learn when they are only playing?

At some point, any caring parent will ask what they believe to be a valid question: How can my children learn when they are only playing? This is a very 'adult' question, because to a five-year-old, learning and play are the same thing. At this point, qualified early years educators are invaluable. They will find the balance, encouraging the child's joy of innate discovery through free play, while also leading them into more structured and relevant learning.

How often do our kids even have the opportunity for free play anymore? Well-meaning parents overprotect them against every perceived threat to their safety, leaving them little space to be the free range kids their parents might have been. In *More Human*,[19] Steve

Hilton explains: 'This over-protective attitude is harming children. Whether it's aggressive bureaucracy removing any remotely challenging play equipment from playgrounds, or panicking over the idea that a child might encounter a single germ or piece of dirt, we are cutting away at the basic humanity of childhood experience'.

Traffic congestion at the start and end of the school day illustrates how cautious we have become. Hilton retells an anecdote from English writer Jay Griffiths in which 'two children, aged eight and five, cycled to school alone and their headmaster threatened to report their parents to social services'.[20] While there are probably at least two sides to this story, it conveys a sense of the cocooning we subject children to today.

A further concern is the loss of the physical exercise that comes with cycling or walking to school. Physical play and exercise are essential for growing bodies. We have to be concerned when schools and governments cut down on physical education lessons to find more time for academic work. Physical activity invigorates both the body and the brain. If we want children's brains to function well, we need to organise regular exercise and free play for them.

A University of Illinois study[21] indicates that children who spend 70 minutes a day running around and playing experience increased brain activity and improved test results. If the weather or politics militate against this physical activity, then perhaps we need a cycling machine at home or at school. If that cannot be done, then consider investing in a standing desk for each child. If nothing else, let them stand whenever they feel the need to stretch. At least their posture will improve.

Computer games deserve to be considered in a discussion about play. Some game environments, such as Minecraft, encourage critical and creative thinking, and are obviously enjoyed by many young players. However, of greater value to a parent is an understanding of gamification,[22] which explores why computer games are so compelling to children, then applies similar principles to other aspects of their lives.

A great computer game offers a sense of challenge, a degree of decision making, an expectation of mastery, and the opportunity to create new ideas and scenarios. These elements are evident in a broad range of successful life experiences, including many for adults. It's not just kids who like to play and learn. Airline frequent flyer programs, through which travellers can build up points and qualify for rewards, were an early example of gamification.

A gamified family is an exciting place for a child. In such an environment, parents offer their children lots of creative challenges and decision-making opportunities, a sense of achievement as they master a skill, and especially, the opportunity to create new ideas and possibilities. So how can we develop this creative skillset in children?

IGNITING THEIR CREATIVE GENIUS

Imagine a daily newspaper that has citronella oil mixed with its printer ink. This might make more sense to you if you lived in a tropical country plagued by mosquitoes and dengue fever. In 2014, the *Mawbima* newspaper in Sri Lanka became a natural mosquito repellent whenever readers opened its pages.[23] This creative solution generated so much interest that it led to a rise in sales of the newspaper.

Your children may have little demand for this application, although they will always need to apply some form of creative thinking in their lives. Over the next decades, creativity will become an increasingly prized skill, given that non-creative organisational thinking will predominantly be done by the artificial intelligence. So how do we develop this creative genius in their lives?

In *Where Good Ideas Come From*, Steven Johnson outlines a series of elements that lead to creative thought. The first is the 'adjacent possible', which means that ideas will be bound by what is available in the world at that time. Virtual reality had no chance of being invented 100 years ago, because none of the supporting technology existed then. Another creative element is referred to as the 'slow hunch'. Some ideas simply take a long time to ferment and come together.

Serendipity is a further element. It is the gift of the happy discovery, the accidental connection that somehow appears in a child's line of sight or thinking. While this might seem to be entirely random, you can increase the possibilities of it occurring by involving them in different, quirky activities that are outside their normal experience. Error, Johnson points out, can also lead to many creative insights. Adults sometimes struggle with children making mistakes, although to learn and create something new, a child first needs to go through lots of trial and error.

While perfectionism can drive children to seek higher standards, paradoxically it can also impede their progress through a determination to avoid making mistakes. Help them to strive instead for excellence, in which they aim for high standards while accepting they will make errors along their learning journey. The early stages of developing new ideas are invariably littered with blunders. Those mistakes are often the best stepping-stones to developing the final product.

> Heading into the future, creativity will take on different dimensions.

Heading into the future, creativity will take on different dimensions. The Maker Movement[24] is gaining momentum as a social response to today's bland stream of mass-produced activities and commodities. This movement brings together an eclectic mix of computer gurus and traditional artisans who use modern design to invent and construct new things.

Hundreds of thousands of people around the world attend Maker Faires, a technological version of farmer's markets. The organisers of the Maker Faire near San Francisco refer to the event as the 'greatest show and tell on Earth'. This will make sense to any school student today.

The Maker Movement is popular in schools and local communities. Makers get together in makerspaces,[25] school or community centres where people of all ages can engage in hands-on learning, design and construction. The Maker Movement is partly a response to learning approaches that too often tied children to pen and paper, or a screen, without involving them in physically creating anything. Designing a model plane simply by drawing, or touching a screen on an iPad, will rarely develop fine motor skills or generate a sense of accomplishment that truly excites a young child.

Encourage children to design something new and intriguing. Give them some enjoyable and simple strategies for creating what they have designed. I once wrote a program called Thinkers Keys[26] that included lots of practical strategies for teaching children to think. One, called the BAR Key[27] (an acronym for Bigger–Add–Replace), outlined simple steps for redesigning an object.

For example, in designing a new TV, they might create a remote control with *bigger* buttons for visually impaired people, then *add* voice-activated robot legs that would move the TV to different parts of the room, and finally *replace* the standard 2D TV shows with an immersive 3D experience.

About ten years ago, a teacher in Hong Kong showed me a BAR design for a new type of shoe drawn by a nine-year-old boy in her class. Its resemblance to the recently released 'Sole Power' shoe[28] is uncanny. This innovative shoe can charge your smartphone using the kinetic energy generated by your walking. I sometimes wonder if that nine-year-old was involved in the Sole Power design phase. We need more creative thinkers like him.

The Combination Key is another strategy that unearths the most remarkable ideas. The aim is to design an entirely new product by combining two objects that normally have nothing to do with each other. I once worked with some schoolchildren who lived near the beach, and we brainstormed ideas for one child's uncle who hired out surfboards. His uncle's problem, the boy explained, was that the hirers pretended not to hear the signal when their time was up.

TALKING WITH THE NEXT GENERATION

WHEN THEY SAY

'I'm not an entrepreneur. I have no idea how to create my own ideas for my life up ahead.'

SOME RESPONSES YOU MIGHT OFFER

'Being an entrepreneur doesn't mean you have to become the next Mark Zuckerberg. Most of us will never set up our own multinational company. **What matters is that you are entrepreneurial in whatever you do,** whether it's in a small part-time job or a service that you're providing through an online site such as TaskRabbit or Fiverr. It means you are prepared to make things happen yourself, rather than waiting for someone else to get things started.'

'**Everyone is creative. Some people just believe it more than others.** Remember that creative ideas may just take a bit of time to generate. Surround yourself with interesting people. Get involved in stimulating experiences. Generate some really ridiculous ideas that stretch your thinking. That extension often leads to other really worthwhile ideas.'

'Some people say that everything possible has now been invented, but they've been saying that for a long time. And they will still be saying it when you're much older. So **set out to become the inventor of something that has never been seen or thought of before.** There are millions of future ideas just waiting for someone like you to introduce them to the world.'

We began to choose all sorts of disparate objects that could be combined with surfboards in some way to resolve this issue. One such item was an iceblock. Easy, said the child. We'll make surfboards out of blocks of ice, and after about an hour they'll just melt away. Then there will be no need to call the hirer back to the shore.

The world will always need those who can think of a melting surfboard, or Play-Doh, or graphic street art, or a stirring piece of music, or a comedy show that makes us laugh out aloud. Who would want to live in a soulless environment without these touches of genius? In the mid 21st century, our children will need such talents more than ever. You can plant those creative seeds today by encouraging your children to be entrepreneurial.

RAISING THE FAMILY ENTREPRENEUR

Twelve-year-old Angie is passionate about her hand-painted cards. She makes around $30 a week from her small stall at the weekend farmer's market. Evan, of EvanTube fame,[29] makes over $1.3 million each year. When he was eight years old, he launched his own YouTube channel with the support of his father. He simply talks about things that would appeal to children his own age, such as in his reviews on the latest computer games.

You will find junior entrepreneurs around the world involved in an endless range of creative and entertaining projects. While it is all very well to turn a profit, the point is not necessarily to become a millionaire by the age of 15. The core benefit is to develop initiative and personal responsibility, and a belief in their own capacity for making things happen. The life lessons involved in creating a product or service, and discovering how to respect their customers, will prepare them for a world that wants and values their enterprise.

We can't protect children from criticism of any poor work they do.

What are the first steps in generating this enterprise? Remember that not all entrepreneurs are wildly creative.

Many of their initiatives are a logical extension of what already exists. Opportunities are all around children. Pets need to be minded when a neighbour is away. I once paid $10 to a teenager for painting street numbers on my rubbish bins. It took him five minutes.

Encourage children to design things—from cards to T-shirts to dog collars. Prompt them to make presents of their own design, rather than buying them. Most recipients of gifts prefer the personal effort that has been expended in creating them. Challenge children to become competent at something, and to be recognised for that talent among their peers. As they build up their list of entrepreneurial options, ask them to compile an Ideas File full of future possibilities. It will prove to be fascinating reading, and a stimulus for further initiatives when they get older.

Working through you, they might even register at sites such as fiverr.com, and provide services that involve graphic art or online research. They will quickly find out whether their work standard is acceptable through the direct feedback they receive from those who have paid for the service. We can't protect children from criticism of any poor work they do. On the contrary, they need to hear it more often, as long as it is offered respectfully.

Some children may make the mistake of believing that any standard of work will suffice when they do a task. At some point, they will receive a shock when they discover that this is not the case. What a wonderful lesson for these children to learn at an early stage, given that one day they may need to create their own employment.

For children who are passionate about their entrepreneurial project, design thinking is an exciting process to build into their planning. There are usually five stages to designing a new idea: empathising, defining, ideating, developing a prototype, testing. Let's use Angie's hand-painted cards as an example.

She first empathised with her mother's frustration at not finding a suitable birthday card for some friends. By talking with her mother and other adults, Angie defined the sort of card that would appeal to them. Next came the ideating or brainstorming of suitable options for her new cards. From there she developed some early prototypes. Finally, in the testing stage, she asked for feedback from others and further refined her designs.

During their formative years, some children become involved in endless design projects. Others become entranced by a single initiative and may eventually become very competent with that project material. Both approaches are very worthwhile.

Regardless of which direction they choose, challenge them to think of the difference they might make in the lives of others with their product or service. Then ask them how they could direct some of their small profit to a worthwhile cause. Entrepreneurship is not meant to selfishly generate massive individual wealth. It is an opportunity for children to contribute to the collective future quality of life.

CHAPTER 8

A helping hand: supporting future philanthropy

WHAT IT'S ABOUT

While reducing poverty and increasing global equity are rarified principles, tomorrow's adults will build these goals into their everyday actions. This chapter outlines many exciting local and global initiatives that will transform philanthropy worldwide. Let's begin with a simple idea: small amounts of cash are the best option to support people in need.

#philanthropy #dispellingthemyths #onlinephilanthropy #juniorphilanthropists

PHILANTHROPY CAN MAKE THE WORLD A BETTER PLACE

Can a one-dollar purchase make a difference to someone's life? Marc Cole discovered that it can. Travelling through Asia in 1989, he met a Tibetan woman suffering from a deadly ear infection and discovered he was able to save her life with a dollar's worth of antibiotics. Later he purchased a $30 hearing aid that restored her hearing. On returning home, he wrote to 100 friends, and asked for donations that would allow him to keep giving small, effective amounts during his travels.

His '100 Friends' charity[1] has since allocated more than $600 000 directly to individuals in 23 countries. As Marc has discovered, there is huge merit to providing small amounts of cash to those in need. One study found that direct cash transfers helped at least 20 per cent more people than food aid.[2] Poorer people in real need know how to use cash for the most economical possible purchases.

More than 10 million non-profit organisations are dedicated to giving support where it is needed around the planet. Philanthropy, broadly, denotes our desire to support the wellbeing of others. The scale of philanthropic organisations ranges from local groups much smaller than 100 Friends to international aid agencies with thousands of employees and volunteers. These efforts are complemented by billions of well-meaning individuals who offer assistance to those around them whenever they can.

> Nearly one-third of the world's population donate to charity, and close to a quarter have volunteered.

According to the 2015 CAF World Giving Index,[3] nearly one-third (31.5 per cent) of the world's population donated to charity, and close to one-quarter (24 per cent) volunteered. Without this vast support, many service organisations and non-profit charities would be unable to survive. The world is already a better place because of this support. The possibilities for our children's future are even more exciting.

Back in 2014, Bill Gates predicted there will be almost no poor countries left in the world by 2035.[4] If he is proved correct—and he is better qualified than most to make such an assessment—it will be in part because of the work of countless non-profit organisations. And it will have a significant positive impact on the futures of children in every country, including yours.

When people in poorer countries achieve a higher standard of living, this creates a healthier economy that benefits world trade. In an improved economy, they generate new ideas and inventions that can advance all of humanity. They are less likely to develop terrorist hotspots, which are too often fuelled by rampant poverty. Over time, they can even move from being recipient nations to becoming donor nations that support others.

Poorer countries and individuals cannot always rise out of poverty by themselves. They often need initial support from philanthropic individuals and charitable organisations to improve their living conditions. Many massive projects have impacted positively on poor nations. Deaths from malaria have been lowered with targeted programs. Teenage pregnancy rates have dropped because of effective education programs, which have also led to improved futures for many of those youth. In the quest to reduce infant malnutrition, long-term farming programs have increased crop yields and improved life expectancy.

Share the many philanthropic success stories with children. You could start by telling them about Room to Read.[5] This non-profit organisation has one outcome in mind: to teach all girls how to read. Room to Read believe that many of the world's problems will be resolved through the provision of a decent education for all girls. Nearly 800 million young people and adults still cannot read, and two-thirds of them are women and girls. Room to Read have trained more than 9000 teachers and librarians, and distributed over 18 million books, and nearly 10 million children have benefited from their programs.

If your children have ever been lucky enough to travel internationally, they may be familiar with another simple project called Change for Good.[6] In this partnership between UNICEF and 12 international airlines, travellers donate loose change they cannot use once they return home. Most of that spare foreign cash would have sat in a home cupboard for years or have been thrown away. Change for Good has raised more than $150 million with that loose change since 1987, the funds allocated to the goal of lowering the number of preventable childhood deaths around the world each day from 16 000 to zero.

Through projects like these, philanthropy can make the world a better place. But does it really always work? While this book focuses wholeheartedly on the best that the world can be, the truthful answer to this question is sobering: it depends.[7] Poorly implemented and expensive projects have sometimes made a local situation worse. Sending tractors to Africa without considering the need for servicing and spare parts can end up making life more complicated for poor farmers. Here are some powerful guidelines that philanthropists everywhere might consider:

◊ Swallow your ego and pride, and team up with other groups who do similar work. Often, too many small charities compete for insufficient funds in the same field.

◊ Focus on direct cash allocations. In many cases, they are more economical.

◊ If you send resources such as books to a region, check that you are not compromising a local small business that relies on book sales.

◊ Ask people what they want. Don't arrogantly presume you know what they need.

◊ Do your research. Find out what else has already been done—what worked, and why; what didn't work, and why.

◊ Focus on helping recipients to develop skills, rather than only on the allocation of resources. Once they have the skills, local people will be able to create the resources for themselves.

◊ Remember, it is always a two-way street. You may learn more from them than they learn from you. Stay open to learning experiences.

When children get involved in supporting others, point out that they are gaining from the experience themselves, not just helping the other person. Acting egotistically as the knight in shining armour is not acceptable. We need to develop balanced relationships that pay respect to both parties. To do this, we need to dispel some age-old myths that too often compromise our ability to help others.

DISPELLING THE MYTHS ABOUT PHILANTHROPY

Urban myths are entertaining at parties. Storytellers will often add their own whimsical gloss to the tale. A human tooth will dissolve if left in a soft drink overnight. The moon landings were a hoax staged by NASA and the US government. There is no shortage of these myths in everyday life, and unfortunately some people choose to believe them.

There are plenty of myths in the world of philanthropy too, although these can have much more serious human consequences. One of the most powerful conversations we can have with our children is the one in which we dispel these inaccurate beliefs. If we don't discuss these things with them, they may be less likely to support worthwhile causes in their adult life.

In his 2014 Bill and Melinda Gates Foundation annual letter, the world's foremost philanthropist outlined three core myths that block progress at the global level.[8] The first is that poor countries are doomed to stay poor. That seemed to be true for many destitute nations in the mid 20th century. In the past 50 years, we have seen remarkable progress, however, especially in Africa.

Seven of the 10 fastest-growing economies of the past half-decade are on the African continent. Since 1970, the percentage of African children in school has grown from the low forties to over 75 per cent. By any measure, poverty has decreased worldwide. Since 1960, China's real income per person has increased eightfold, while India's has grown fourfold. One mistaken belief is that aid creates dependency. On the contrary, the history of the early 21st century tells us that aid leads to independence.

The second myth is that foreign aid is a big waste. There was some truth in that even in the late 20th century, when stories of aid money being diverted to line political leaders' pockets were common. With more open accountability, created in part by the internet, this is now highly unlikely. In any case, no first-world nation ever spends anything like 10 per cent of their budget on foreign aid; in most cases, it is well below 1 per cent.

At the time of writing, the United States offered just 0.19 per cent of its national income, although this was likely to plummet under the Trump administration. The Australian figure is 0.27 per cent. A group of OECD countries have set a target of 0.7 per cent, and this has been matched or exceeded by Norway, Sweden, Denmark, Luxembourg and now the UK.[9]

The third philanthropy myth is that saving lives will lead to overpopulation. On the contrary, the rate of increase in population slows down when lives are saved. When economic conditions improve, medical services advance and the infant mortality rate is lowered. When parents know that more of their children will live into adulthood, they have fewer of them. Women in poorer countries also have greater access to birth control today, and can make choices about the number of children they have. The world's population is growing more slowly each year. Will our children's future be ravaged by global overpopulation? Not if these trends continue.

There are also some everyday myths about local philanthropy. You have undoubtedly heard this one from a social commentator: 'Only a small percentage of my donation gets to the people who need the support'. The reality? Yes, some of your money must be used for administrative purposes such as wages, rent, equipment and electricity bills. How else can the organisation arrange to deliver their services? Part of your contribution is meant to pay for their administration.

Even in philanthropic organisations, volunteers cannot be expected to do everything. We need professionals who can apply their years of experience to the task, and they deserve to be paid. At the same time, charities need to develop exceptional standards of accountability. One rule-of-thumb is that one-third of all funds will be devoted to overheads, although specific circumstances such as an isolated location may alter that allocation.

Some donors also express concern about scam merchants who claim to be a charity. The reality? Yes, such behaviour does occasionally occur, and it pays to research a charity properly before you offer it support.[10] Teach children to cross-reference their findings when they are checking out an organisation, performing at least two different searches. Check out the ratings on social media: if there are only a couple of ratings, they are probably not to be relied on. If thousands have given them a single star out of five, there may be strong reasons for avoiding them. A CEO who is driving a late-model Ferrari sends an incongruous message, and you might reconsider your support.

The issue of 'fake news' came to public notice in the early Trump era.[11] This fake news development is a clear signal that we must teach our children how to discern what is 'true' and what may be a myth. Back in the 20th century, there was some degree of trust in the TV anchor newsreader making an effort to share the verifiable truth. Also, your neighbours heard the same news as you, which provided a common reference point for everyone.

> This fake news development is a clear signal that we must teach our children how to discern what is 'true' and what may be a myth.

The influence of 'fake news' has changed all that. While social media has many merits, it also allows anyone online to manipulate the truth and even just make things up. A political group may end up using fake stories to reinforce its agenda. As an example, a government intent on slashing aid funding may pick up a social media rumour about wastage in previous programs, and release it as a 'fact'.

Socrates' famous 'Test of Three'[12] is a useful response to fake news. When approached with gossip or rumour, the great philosopher would ask three questions. The first question: 'Do you absolutely know that this is true?' If the answer was no or maybe, he would request that the conversation stop there. If yes, then the second question was: 'Is it something good about the person involved?' Again, a no would halt the dialogue. The third question was then: 'Is it useful for me to know it?' True, good and useful. The world would be a better place without gossip, fabrication and innuendo. Consider applying the Test of Three in your family dialogue.

IMPLEMENTING ONLINE PHILANTHROPY

If he was alive today, Socrates' response to our online world would be interesting. While its collective propensity for gossip and innuendo might have exhausted him, even he would have acknowledged its philanthropic benefits. News of a major disaster can reach half of the world's population within seconds, and a fundraising appeal will often have begun within the hour. On Wednesday, 24 August 2015, a 6.2 earthquake struck central Italy and left at least 267 people dead. A number of small towns were devastated by the tragedy.

Online news bulletins immediately carried links for donations to reputable charities in the region that were qualified to offer support. Within two days, Italian restaurants around the world were offering a dish called Pasta Amatriciana, a pasta dish from Amatrice, which was one of the smaller towns that had been destroyed. Each sale of the dish around the world meant a donation of two euros to the appeal.[13]

Welcome to the world of cyber-philanthropy, or what some refer to as *clicktivism*.[14] With the touch of a few buttons on a mobile phone, you can donate to a crowdfunding project, or join or even organise a boycott or protest. Online petitions through such sites as change.org and avaaz.org are popular. Clicktivism has plenty of benefits. It promotes awareness of issues, and it can lead to higher rates of donation to worthwhile causes. Not everyone is happy about the process, however.

Some critics refer to it as *slacktivism*, and claim that social activism today has been reduced to a barrage of meaningless 'likes' and the signing of interminable petitions that require no more than a single click in a box. Authentic involvement, according to these critics, is undermined by this trend. Still, it needs to be asked: what is it that gives the best possible support to the cause in question?

If the answer is funding, then most charities will be happy. Online fundraising has dramatically simplified the process of donating to a cause, and our children will increasingly contribute online. Already, Charitweet makes donating as easy as a couple of clicks on Twitter. You tweet to a charity that you wish to offer them a donation, and they send you a link to their payment website.[15] Fundraising expenses are lowered by these donations being sent online.

Lunchbox[16] also makes the donation process easy. This small cash transaction device sits on shop and business counters all over London. A quick tap by a customer leads to a 30p donation for lunches for children in poor countries. When you tap your card, you receive a visual and sound cue that thanks you for your donation. Already 15 000 children in countries such as South Sudan, Ecuador and Haiti have received lunches from Lunchbox.

> A quick tap by a customer leads to a 30p donation for lunches for children in poor countries.

Since the beginning of this century, crowdfunding has revolutionised the way individuals can raise much-needed capital for inspiring causes. With crowdfunding, you receive funding from online supporters in various ways including direct lending, equity funding and outright donation. Early critics dismissed it as a passing fad, although its progress shows no signs of slowing. In 2015, equity crowdfunding raised more than $34 billion worldwide, which is over 12 times the amount raised just three years earlier. The industry is expected to grow to over $300 billion by 2025.[17]

Crowdfunding can be a great way to get a worthwhile philanthropic project started. For example, an innovative device called the Community Chlorine Maker easily passed its funding target of $50 000 in December 2016. Using only water, salt and a battery, it creates chlorine to treat tainted water. A donation of $160 by a supporter covered the cost of one device that would service 200 people or more.[18]

Philanthropic activity features strongly on many crowdfunding platforms. Some are devoted exclusively to specific causes. Kangu[19] allows you to make donations that support healthcare for expectant mothers and newborn babies in countries with inadequate medical services. An Australian non-profit foundation called School Aid has created the world's first crowdfunding platform for children who want to raise funds specifically for a social justice cause[20]. Since its inception, School Aid has raised more than $5 million for disaster relief around the world. This money has been raised specifically by and for children. Their inspiring premise is: Helping kids change their world.

On Kiva,[21] you can loan a small amount of money to a budding entrepreneur in a developing country. Those loans might support a Peruvian coffee farmer who wants to use organic fertiliser, or a Kenyan woman who needs to pay her start-up university fees. Over 97 per cent of all loans have been repaid. The micro-financing concept was first implemented by Bangladesh's Grameen Bank in 1983.

New philanthropic opportunities constantly emerge as a result of updated technologies. For example, 80 per cent of amputees around the world do not have access to modern prosthetics. Enabling the Future[22] is a worldwide network of volunteers who use 3D printing to help the amputee to create a prosthetic hand. If you have a 3D printer, they will offer instruction on how to proceed. If you don't have a 3D printer, they will find someone who lives nearby to print it for you.

The UNICEF Tap Project, held in March each year, encourages you to take a break from your phone.[23] Their app tracks your downtime, and for every 15 minutes of your digital detox, the sponsors will pay for a day's supply of clean drinking water for a child in a developing country. In 2014, 2.6 million participants in 26 countries generated over $1 million in clean water funding.

Wearable technologies may encourage children to become more philanthropically involved. The Kid Power Band[24] is a type of Fitbit wristband that promotes fitness in children and retails for $40. Each step they take earns points recorded in an app, with the points converting into nutrition packs for undernourished children in poor countries; 12000 steps a day translates into five food packs. In October 2014, 900 students in Sacramento earned enough points to provide a full treatment course for 473 badly malnourished children. Just imagine what other creative initiatives the world will eventually create.

A FUTURE FOR PHILANTHROPY

While some future initiatives may be beyond our imagination for now, we can be confident that someone's children will eventually bring them to life. So what can we do to create a thriving philanthropic world that encourages these imaginative possibilities? Three powerful implementations will make all the difference to our children's future world of giving.

1. Positive deviancy

Positive deviancy is the important first step, and rest assured that it is indeed positive and it has nothing to do with immoral behaviour. It refers to the different thinking needed when we support people in need. In 1990, a life-changing project in South-East Asia challenged many large philanthropic organisations to adopt this different thinking.[25]

Vietnam was facing near-famine conditions, with two-thirds of its children suffering malnutrition, following the loss of subsidised rice imports and a return to private agriculture. Save the Children had been approached by the Vietnamese government for help in finding a sustainable solution to the child nutrition issue, especially in remote rural areas. The program developers decided to implement a different approach, and rather than giving more handouts, they searched for villagers who were already feeding their children well. These parents had managed to optimise on the scant resources they had. The next step was to arrange for those parents to explain to others what they were doing.

It takes practice to change behaviour, so at dinnertime each day for two weeks the villagers, including the children, gathered at the home of the parents who were feeding their own children well. After six months, the program was so successful that Vietnam duplicated it in a further 250 villages.

This positive deviancy focuses on the strengths in a community and sustains the long-term viability of the change program. Instead of becoming dependent on outside expertise, the local people tapped into their own collective capabilities. This will become a hallmark of mid–21st century philanthropic practice.

2. Entrepreneurial philanthropy

The next step in creating a passionate world of giving is to unleash the ingenuity of all entrepreneurs on the planet, and to direct their energy towards philanthropic causes. We need innovative humanitarians who think differently. The drive for financial and technological success that is evident in Silicon Valley would create an unrivalled world of equity and opportunity in the social justice sector.

How would this be done? Think of *Shark Tank* or the entrepreneur clubs that often feature on mainstream TV, which involve millionaires who ponder the proposals of start-up capitalists. Imagine instead that the wealthy benefactors assess philanthropic proposals and determine which project they would support.

These altruistic mechanisms already exist in many forms. Enterprise philanthropy is frequently practised throughout the world and is represented by hundreds of associations that coordinate the work of different grant-giving groups.[26] Social Ventures Australia (SVA)[27] is a good example of what is called venture philanthropy. SVA provide funding, logistical support and networking opportunities to social purpose organisations. They mediate between the small start-ups and the corporate funders who want to support such ventures.

Wealthy millennials are increasingly seeking ways to invest in philanthropic ventures.[28] And, rather than seeing such involvement as a tax break or an opportunity to boost their social standing, they want to create a sustainable impact with their funding. They are a wonderful model for today's children.

3. Honouring diversity

Thirdly, through their philanthropic work, our children will learn important lessons about honouring diversity. The world encompasses an endless variety of human differences, whether of nationality, ethnicity, religion, skin tone or personal beliefs. Your willingness to respect that diversity signals the quality of your own character.

Our differences are what make us interesting. What a boring world it would be if everyone looked the same and acted in the same way. People travel because they love to experience different people, cultures and places. Difference inspires us, and our children will live richer lives through experiencing this diversity.

> What a boring world it would be if everyone looked the same and acted in the same way.

Not that they will have a choice. The demographic trends indicate that the world will become increasingly diverse. As noted earlier, nearly 90 per cent of today's under-20s live in emerging countries[29] in Africa, the Middle East, South America and Asia. The mid 21st century will be an ethnically different world. The 2015 US Census figures indicated that ethnic minorities now surpass non-Hispanic whites as the biggest group of American children under the age of five.[30]

TALKING WITH THE NEXT GENERATION

WHEN THEY SAY

'It doesn't make sense to help other people everywhere in the world. There are too many, and it's a waste of money anyway. What about us and our own family, let alone our own country?'

SOME RESPONSES YOU MIGHT OFFER

'Of course you need to help your own family as much as possible. However, to give philanthropically to others around the world is also good for you and your family. Here's why. With less global poverty, we are all safer. Stronger economies will develop new markets for the goods and services we create in our own countries. We sometimes call it the Common Good. **What we do for others helps everyone, including ourselves.'**

'It's not a waste of money to make donations to charities. Nearly all of them are very careful with how they use those donations, and the benefits can be easily measured. In the past few decades, many countries have been lifted out of poverty because of the amazing support that has been given to them by richer people and nations.'

'Yes, there are billions of poorer people still in the world. That's a lot of individuals, and it can seem overwhelming to try to help everyone. But each of them is a human being who is like you in so many ways. They play, they learn, they love their parents just like you. **If we are serious about being fair, then we have to help people who are less fortunate than us, whether they are in our own country or elsewhere.'**

Respect for diversity won't just be a choice. It will be a necessity, and targeted philanthropy will be one of the most powerful ways to encourage this diversity. When our children value and implement philanthropy in the future, the chances of eliminating poverty and inequity will increase.

The examples we set for them today will influence the choices they make in two decades from now. This modelling of yours can even guide them right now. With your support, what philanthropic choices might your own children make this week?

RAISING A JUNIOR PHILANTHROPIST

Imagine sitting in front of your whole school assembly as an 11-year-old, and being shaved bald by two tattoo-covered barbers. Digby Bankes did this at his Melbourne primary school in March 2017, after raising $11 000 for Leukaemia Foundation's 'Shave For A Cure'. With rousing cheers echoing from hundreds of students, he fulfilled his desire to support a cause that was dear to his heart. A young age no longer impedes our children from engaging in such activities. On the contrary, they want to make this philanthropic difference, and many know how to do it.

Parental role-modelling matters. When parents are philanthropic, 71 per cent of children become philanthropists themselves as adults, compared with only 47 per cent of children whose parents are not philanthropists.[31] This role-modelling includes activities such as donating regularly, doing volunteering work and, especially, talking with children about social justice causes. With your family, you might sponsor a child in a developing country or wrap Christmas hampers for homeless people. Community clean-ups always need more volunteers.

What else might you do? Collect all your unused or unwanted clothing, and deliver it to a charity that supports homeless people. Volunteer to sit with patients in an aged care facility and listen to their life stories. Collect loose change and place it in a charity collection box on your next shopping trip. Write letters to politicians and ask them to support your favourite cause. Instead of giving birthday or Christmas presents, arrange for a donation in the person's name to a worthwhile charity. Watch out for elderly neighbours who may need occasional support. Set up a small automated donation to a charity that impresses you.

The issue is not whether you will find possible philanthropic activities for your family. There are plenty out there. The issue is whether it matters to you. These choices will depend on your availability of time and your financial status, among other things. They will also depend on your priorities and value system as a parent. How much do altruism and helpfulness matter to you with regard to your children, as compared with diligence and perseverance, or high achievement and outstanding results? Although some might disagree, these different values are not mutually exclusive.

> People like to work with Givers, whose success comes from the trust and goodwill they establish with others.

The disagreement comes from those who argue that you will never compete as a high achiever in life if you are consistently diverting your time and energy to others. Let's clarify this, given how important it is to most parents. Do your children need to avoid helping others to get ahead?

Adam Grant offers some powerful perspectives in *Givers, Takers, and Matchers: The Surprising Psychology of Success*.[32] According to his definitions, Matchers give to others, although only with people they believe will help them in return. Takers are happy to ask for help, although they rarely give anything in response. Givers are intrinsically motivated to help others, without expecting any help in return.

Can you guess which style is the most successful in the workplace? Surprisingly to some, the least successful are the Givers, although only in certain circumstances. Givers can be too easily distracted by the desire to help others, to the detriment of their own work.

Conversely, the most successful are also the Givers, as long as they respect their own work time while supporting others. People like to work with Givers, whose success comes from the trust and goodwill they establish with others. Givers benefit in all areas of life, whether professional or personal.

The value of giving to the receiver is self-evident, although the process also has benefits for the Giver. People who are generous with their money and their time report that they experience 'helper's high' when they support others who are less fortunate than themselves. This experience boosts their brain's endorphins, which creates an exultant sense of wellbeing.[33] They can also experience a sense of gratitude for their own advantages when they see others in more difficult circumstances. The act of giving can even develop deeper social connections.[34]

How would you wish to be remembered for your contribution to society? I've always been interested in eulogies. Not in a macabre sense, but in the respectful and inspiring way that someone's life is encapsulated in a single powerful reading. What will be said in yours? Would you prefer to be recalled as a generous soul who balanced your own needs with those of many others? Your philanthropic efforts will shape what is in your eulogy. And your children will be listening very carefully.

CHAPTER 9

Action stations: fashioning the future right now

WHAT IT'S ABOUT

Actions speak louder than words. This chapter explores a series of exciting action projects and processes that will make a tangible difference to our children's lives, and to the lives of many others, by the mid 21st century. Let's start by considering what is called a 'wicked' problem.

#solutionfocus #problemfinding #incentives #actionprojects #conversation

THE POWER OF SOLUTION

In August 2016, a truck became stuck under the Scitech bridge in Perth, Western Australia.[1] By now, of course, rescuers around the world know how to solve the problem. The origins of this solution are shrouded in mystery, although my favourite version involves the 10-year-old who approached some engineers as they pondered how to dislodge a truck that had become wedged in a tunnel. 'Just let the tyres down,' she offered. And they did.

Solving problems has multiple benefits. It stimulates our creative juices; it generates satisfaction in resolving an issue; it builds better relationships with our partners, family members and friends; it creates community. Implementing a solution gives you the confidence to take on further problems. A mindframe that focuses on solutions ensures a healthier and more productive life.

Not all issues are easily resolved, however. We sometimes encounter what are called 'wicked problems' that are near intractable. In the future, such issues will give our children the opportunity to learn how to resolve a problem that is not easily unravelled. Take, for example, housing affordability in many countries, an issue that will eventually impact on every child today. Let's use this dilemma as an illustration of how to approach a wicked problem.

The problem of housing affordability has reached near-crisis levels for young people in some parts of the world. Around the start of the 21st century, half of the 16- to 35-year age group in London owned their own home. At the time of writing, it was one-quarter and dropping.[2] Sydney median house prices now are up to 12 times the average annual salary, up from four times the annual salary in the 1970s.[3] So what's the real problem?

You might say that it is the high cost of housing, although that is only the end result. For our children to ever resolve a complicated issue like this, they will need to determine the real problem behind the high costs. This is one reason why people don't solve their problems. They end up solving the wrong one. It's not solution-finding we need to do initially. It's problem-finding.

So what's the real problem behind the high cost of housing? Perhaps it can be attributed to poor long-term infrastructure planning for new housing developments; or an unavailability of suitable land for construction; or young people lacking the patience to save for a deposit; or wages for young people not matching the rise in the cost of housing; or young people wanting an expensive house that is way beyond their means; or a society that has reoriented a basic social need such as housing into an investment opportunity, which pushes up the value of property. Take your pick. It is usually a combination of problems.

Each one of these issues is a solution-in-waiting. If patience is the problem, then a discussion with a decent financial planner may be the first step to saving for a deposit. This is assuming that they can indeed save while paying exorbitant rent. However, wicked problems call for wicked and innovative solutions, and there is no shortage of inventive options available to counter the high cost of housing. So what possibilities have already been implemented?

◊ Sometimes called 'IKEA on steroids', micro-housing involves a dramatic downsizing to a single-room abode, complete with fold-away bedrooms and innovative storage options.

◊ Shared purchasing with friends can allow 20-somethings into a tight market. They just need to be very good friends.

◊ Some young people have even crowdfunded for their first property. In 2015, 17-year-old Gold Coast student Caitlan Argyle had set herself a $48 000 goal to cover her deposit, and managed to reach $6125 after two months.[4] So why would someone give her money? She had promised rental accommodation in her new house to all contributors. You have to admire her initiative.

◊ Home-sitting and pet-sitting services abound. Your children may not end up owning a home when they offer these services, although at least they have somewhere to live for free while they are saving for a deposit.

Think ahead. Within the next decade, 3D printed houses and apartments may dramatically lower the cost of construction. Land rather than the building may become the value point, given that buildings will be assembled, disassembled and reassembled quickly in another location. More people may move out of cities when virtual meeting technologies become more advanced, which may influence the cost of housing. It is very possible that global market corrections will influence house and apartment prices.

Some of today's children will become part of the wealthiest generation in human history, given that their investor parents will have acquired several houses plus extensive retirement reserves or superannuation savings. And this bounty will likely be shared between fewer siblings, given the trend towards smaller family sizes. Such prosperity will unfortunately be enjoyed only by the children of the affluent class. These examples of thinking ahead may create very different outcomes for housing affordability and general lifestyle.

Solutions in the 2040s may require dramatic rethinking. Some media commentators argue that today's children will be the first generation in western societies to be worse off than their parents.[5] What does 'worse' mean, though? Are they concerned about a trend for today's children to live in smaller housing? Or work 25 hours instead of 65 hours a week? Or own as little in the way of material possessions as their grandparents? Or have as little debt as their grandparents had? There is some merit to these options. 'Worse' may very well become a matter of perspective.

INCENTIVES FOR GENERATING ACTION

Putting a solution into action is a great incentive for children, although that may not be enough to generate real effort. Many parents and teachers are desperate for ideas on how to motivate children. Here's a reality check for you: don't bother. The entire positive thinking movement needs to be reframed, given its core premise that our positive moods can be flicked on like a switch. Think carefully. When you have to start on something you don't like doing, can you suddenly get yourself authentically enthusiastic about it? If you can't, then how can you expect it of a 10-year-old?

So what can be done about this? Let's look at a specific task: completing a school assignment. It is often attempted at the last minute. Right away, help children to accept the negativity they are initially feeling.[6] Ask them to walk around, take a few breaths, then sit down and work alongside that negativity. Set a 30-minute timer and commit them to working for at least that long.

If nothing else, they might at least get some work done, even if they are not smiling about it. Encourage them just to get started. It's half the battle. We don't need children to be dancing with joy as they take on every one of their tasks in life. What we need is for them just to get started. The momentum can then make it easier to continue.

Breaking a task into smaller chunks can help with getting organised. One of the best pieces of advice I know is 'one bird at a time'. In a delightful little book called *Bird by Bird*,[7] Anne Lamott recounts an occasion when her 10-year-old brother had an assignment on birds that was due the next day.

Parents everywhere will be familiar with this scenario. After having had three months to complete the project, he had left it until the last night. Sitting there forlornly, he felt overwhelmed by the enormity of what he still had to do. His father sat down beside him, put his arm around his shoulder and said, 'Bird by bird, buddy. Just take it bird by bird'.

In situations like this, self-regulatory behaviour in children is critical. If you try to control their thinking and behavioural responses, you will still be doing it when they are 50. Children finally wake up to the world when

> We don't need children to be dancing with joy as they take on every one of their tasks in life.

they understand that they have control over their own thoughts, words and actions, and even their emotions. We help them to gain this control, one bird at a time. In endless small instances over the years, we ask questions such as: What did you do successfully with this task? What are some different options you might try next time?

Author Daniel Pink sees external carrots and sticks as very 20th century. In his book *Drive*,[8] he outlines three core factors necessary for self-motivation. *Autonomy* is our desire to be self-regulated, and to have choice and control over the experience. *Mastery* is the urge to get better at doing something. *Purpose* is the determination to do something that makes a difference to the world.

If only we were able to develop an X-Prize incentive for every child on the planet. It would constantly support those three factors. The X-Prize Foundation[9] offers millions of dollars as motivation to solve some far-reaching global problems. Founder Peter Diamandis maintains that you must harness the crowd to remain competitive,[10] and his organisation has certainly done that.

Here is one example. The Gulf of Mexico oil spill was a tragedy for the communities along the shoreline, and necessity became the mother of invention for cleaning up the ocean. In 2011, the X-Prize Foundation announced a $1.4 million prize, open to anyone in the world, to design a more effective oil clean-up process. The winning solution achieved a 400 per cent improvement over the previous industry standard for the recovery of surface oil.

In the past few years, the X-Prize has created incentives for repeated rocket travel to the moon and improved fuel efficiency in future car design. Some near-future incentive prizes will measurably enhance human civilisation. The Qualcomm Tri-corder X-Prize has led to the development of a portable wireless device for monitoring and diagnosing 13 health conditions, which will be usable anywhere in the world. The Global Learning X-Prize will focus on the development of scalable, open source software that will support children in developing countries to teach themselves basic reading, writing and arithmetic within 18 months.

The X-Prize Foundation has recently announced a special competition for 8- to 17-year-olds[11] to develop a lunar robotic mission. This aligns beautifully with the STEM focus in education worldwide, and will hopefully lead to many other similar incentive prizes for school students. Imagine a world where local communities band together to provide stimulus for student initiative. Rather than prize money, the children might vie for access to mentoring from high-profile people or to engagement in an outstanding learning experience.

TALKING WITH THE NEXT GENERATION

WHEN THEY SAY

'It's hard work to do a big project. Is it really worth it?'

SOME RESPONSES YOU MIGHT OFFER

'**We all need some purpose in our lives.** It gives us something to live for. And getting involved in a project is one fantastic way to discover that purpose. Think about the anticipation you feel when you wake up in the morning and you have an exciting task to work on during the day. Imagine feeling that way every day of your life.'

'**Once you taste success, you will never look back.** The first time you put a project into action, you will realise that you can do the same with other projects, again and again. These skills will benefit you for the rest of your life, whether in your work or your volunteering or your personal life.'

'The projects in your life often solve problems. They might be yours or someone else's. **It's much more fun to be the sort of person who solves problems, rather than someone who complains about them.** Other people will prefer to be around you as well, because you are more optimistic about everything in your life.'

Citizen science[12] is another incentive that attracts millions of passionate participants. Sometimes referred to as crowdsourcing for amateur scientists, it harnesses the power of the web to engage enthusiasts worldwide in collecting and analysing data. For example, GlobalXplorer[13] invites people to analyse satellite images currently available to archaeologists, and to report previously undiscovered sites. As well, observers are asked to share evidence that looting may have taken place in valuable locations.

Zooniverse[14] is the world's biggest platform for this kind of people-powered research. At any one time, it can feature 50 or more citizen science projects, ranging from the mapping of changes in animal habitats to the classification of distant galaxies. Can you imagine a 10-year-old budding scientist's reaction when she is the first person to find a previously undiscovered galaxy? That thrill of discovery may fuel a lifetime of exploration. Smart adults don't tell children to get motivated. They involve them in activities such as citizen science that fuel the child's own interest.

FINDING PURPOSE WITH ACTION PROJECTS

A specific action project is a child's implementation of something that excites them. An action project might address a question such as: How can we code our pet robot to sing? It might be a hobby that involves the intricate construction of a model plane or car. Or the action project might revolve around fundraising for a disabled friend who needs a secondhand wheelchair.

While it may be a one-day intensive effort, most action projects last much longer. These projects encourage commitment and help the children to understand that many great achievements in life need consistent long-term effort. Ask them to set 100-day goals rather than three-month goals, or 20-day goals instead of three-week goals. The numbers appeal more to children and add a touch of excitement as the countdown continues. An action project may be an individual effort or completed as a team. It weaves together makerspaces, entrepreneurship and initiative into a single venture.

Children are often taught a process for working through their project, which is critical for young people who have little idea how to organise their thinking. In chapter 6, we introduced an inquiry process, which is used when a child wants to learn more about a topic. The design process in chapter 8 is applied to the creation of a new idea. The action process is about making something happen.

Let's use a project as an example. Charlie and his friends want to raise money to buy a secondhand wheelchair for a disabled classmate. Like most kids, they want to just rush into doing something. The dilemma is that, halfway through those actions, they realise that they haven't properly thought through what they need to do, and the action falls apart.

> When children know that someone else will see their work, it drives their efforts.

So encourage them to go through the following process. This is drawn from my Thinkers Keys material. There are five clear stages, each of which involves a series of questions. Not every question needs a response, although at least one question needs to be addressed at each stage. Here we go:

1. **The Purpose Key**

   ◊ Why are we doing this project?

   ◊ Why is it so important to us?

   ◊ What do we want to achieve?

2. **The Info Key**

   ◊ What background information do we need to find out before we start?

   ◊ Who would know the information we need to find out?

3. The Brainstorming Key

◊ What options are possible?

◊ What has been done before?

◊ What are some really creative and edgy ideas?

4. The Decision Key

◊ Which of these ideas might be the best ones to do?

◊ Which idea/s will we put into action?

5. The Action Key

◊ How and when will we do this?

◊ Who will do what?

◊ What's the timeline for each action?

◊ What are the success indicators for each action?

In the final stage, they often share their completed work with others, who get to see the result of their efforts. When children know that someone else will see their work, it drives their efforts. Like people of all ages, they rebel against doing something that they perceive has no purpose. In this case, the end result is the core purpose for doing the project.

Having a purpose—or a series of purposes—in life really matters. One commonly expressed concern is that children today lack a raison d'être, a reason for being, although this probably applies to a fair proportion of adults as well. Long-term worry or anxiety, and even suicide, are sometimes attributed in part to this lack of purpose.

So where do we find this raison d'être? It seems to come from having something greater than ourselves in our lives. It may be God, or our devotion to a cause, or the inspiration we get from working diligently and achieving a goal. We all need something to live for. Action projects can offer that purpose ... and then we get to celebrate our success.

CELEBRATING THEIR ACHIEVEMENTS

We can learn a lot of things from sport. As well as all of the obvious lessons about fitness, teamwork and perseverance, perhaps the most exciting one is the way we celebrate a win by our favourite team. I have attended grand finals where the home team has won and the post-match emotion floods the stadium.

If only we celebrated our academic and literary achievements with the same energy. Just imagine how it would inspire a 14-year-old if her breakthrough science competition win was cheered wildly at her school assembly. What if Charlie and his friends hit their fundraising target for the wheelchair purchase, and received the same response? Admittedly, given their ages, they would probably be embarrassed by the adulation.

We all need to consider doing some celebrating in our own life. When was the last time you celebrated a success in your life? Equally importantly, when did you really celebrate a success that your children experienced? If your answer is, 'Hmmm, I'm not sure,' then perhaps you need to think about whether your life is missing that vital final ingredient: the one where you celebrate achievement.

Why not have a Friday night family celebration of everyone's successes during the week? You might need to clarify what constitutes a success. Simply performing what is expected of them anyway, such as attending school, hardly represents an outstanding success for most. Contributing to a lunchtime club that supports a charity is another matter. When a weekly process like this is set up in the family, it encourages children to reflect on their successes, and even to seek out new ones.

It's easy to denigrate the 'selfie' idea, although there may be merit in using those self-shots to reinforce these successes. A 10-second video interview of your children might be the perfect process for demonstrating an exciting achievement during that Friday celebratory sharing. Remember that we are talking about 'screenagers' here. Many of them have featured on Facebook, rightly or wrongly, since the day they were born, so they know how to show others what they have done.

In their adulthood, today's generation will be able to access the most comprehensive database of their achievements in history. The old photo album of the 20th century has been supplanted by a comprehensive collation of image and video documenting their lives. Take advantage of this. Consider using apps such as 365 Days that store one image a day. A similar process can be used for short videos. An app called 1 Second Everyday will stitch those short videos together, so an entire year of their life can be watched in just six minutes.

Perhaps a giant visual montage might be placed on the lounge room wall, featuring a family image from every day of your collective lives. If one image or video every day is too much for your organising capabilities, then think about placing one up there every week. All of these collations help you to remember and celebrate what is special about your achievements. Given their highly attuned visual memories, children will remember what happened on a particular day just by revisiting the respective image.

> We all need to consider doing some celebrating in our own life.

Life can be lived at a rapid pace, and most of what occurs is quickly forgotten. Can you remember what you were doing on 24 May last year? There is merit in the daily scrapbooking of what children have experienced. The process is not necessarily just about applauding their achievements. It is also about impressing on them the value of what they are offering to others, and understanding that life is a celebration of what we have experienced.

All around the world, billions of people are storing these representations of their lives, and media organisations are doing likewise with our collective experiences. I love the collations that summarise what the world has achieved in the past 12 months. Searching for 'the 10 greatest science discoveries of the year' or 'the best non-profits of the year' will unearth a wonderful list of achievements. It helps to bring home to us that we accomplish so much that is extraordinary in each passing year.

Of course, there are those who look for the worst as well. One of the more absurd headlines in living memory featured on the web at the end of 2016: '14 reasons why 2016 was the worst year ever'. Really? Someone is a poor student of history. Each year from now on, perhaps we need a mandatory headline that proclaims: 'Why this was the best year ever'. Here's a guarantee: whoever produces that story will always find an endless list of things to write about.

All through this book, I have challenged us to look for what is done well, and to continue with that great work. As we accomplish one impressive achievement after another, let's congratulate ourselves. We don't need to party outrageously every day. Sometimes our celebration may be little more than a quiet reflection on the worth of the project.

The intriguing thing is that, in some ways, it's not that complicated to find satisfaction in everyday existence based on celebration and gratitude. Life itself is so daily. Nothing really changes in our lives until we change what we do each day. Much is made of grand plans and projections for the future, but the measure of our success is in our everyday routine. And there is one special set of experiences that draws all of those daily efforts together: it is the conversations we have with each other.

THE FUTURE DEFINED BY TODAY'S WORDS

On average, we each speak about 16 000 words every day, although that can depend on our work and our personality. The number of words we use is not determined by whether we are male or female. Contrary to the opinion of some, women do not speak more than men.[15]

However many words we say, write or text, where does our choice of those words fit on a line between solutions and problems? Between respect and disparagement? Between gratitude and ingratitude? The words we use clearly indicate our character. They also have the most important influence on how we raise beautiful kids, given that words are our core mode of communication.

The words we use—spoken and written—shape the world. Imagine if we recorded the trillions of words that are used every day and rated them on a massive algorithm from one to ten, from problem to solution. That scale would reflect global thinking, and would indicate the actions we are collectively more likely to take up ahead. Our children's future is being determined right now by the words being used in all of that communication. Your next words add to this total.

There is life-changing power in every conversation you have with a child. You are modelling your own oral language, you are shaping their beliefs about the world, and you are signalling your support for their welfare. In their adult years, they will remind you of the time you said some special words to them when they were eight years old. Words live on in their memory, and contribute to the sum total of their development.

So what can be done when others want to disparage the world today? Consider this scenario. You are at a family gathering, and someone begins to complain about incompetent politicians or refugees or badly behaved teenagers. No solutions are being offered. These negative diatribes are fuelled by a lifetime practice of looking for what is wrong with the world, without ever offering a worthwhile solution. The modelling to children present in the room is hardly positive.

Becoming embroiled in an argument means that no one will win, and often that everyone will lose badly. The person may be melancholic or even depressive, which requires respect and tact. One option is to offer an engaging story that demonstrates the success of a particular practice. Refer to real people when you can. It gives authenticity and coherence to the story. If the complaint was about refugees, then tell a story about a refugee who has achieved success.

If there is one thing you can almost guarantee when people congregate, it is that they love to listen to great stories.

> Hope gives children the belief that they can make great things happen.

In a world that is facing many complexities, let's choose words and stories that create the future we want for our children. The choices are stark. If your teenager is about to go out into the world of work, which conversation topic at that family gathering is more supportive of her? The statistics on long-term unemployment in the local area? Or the local businesses who have banded together to guarantee employment for school leavers?

Your skill at the family gathering is to slowly redirect the conversation, without appearing to disrespect the negative opinions. Look for the stories that encourage children into taking optimistic action. After having a couple of drinks at that gathering, some adults may forget that their children are listening to the conversations. They are, and what they hear is slowly shaping their perspective about the future. We all need to engage in conversations filled with hope.

Those children need that hope to take into the world up ahead. Hopeful individuals see barriers in life as challenges to be overcome,[16] and are more likely to make the effort to resolve the issues. Hope is based on the belief that something worthwhile awaits us up ahead. Hope springs eternal, and fuels an interest in staying alive. In the 19th century, Emily Dickinson wrote, 'Hope is the thing with feathers / that perches in the soul / and sings the tunes without the words / and never stops at all'.

We all need to keep the singing going. If it's not us today, then who is responsible for creating hope for the world up ahead? Hope is all about the future. Hope gives children the belief that they can make great things happen. The future, 20 years from now, is shaped by what everyone talks about today. 'Everyone' means every one, including you and me.

Gratitude is just as critical. It is the past and the present. Feeling grateful generates a sense of wonder at what has already been accomplished in the world, and at what is being achieved today. When both gratitude and hope are present in our children's lives, they are more likely to believe that their future is determined by *choices* they can make, rather than *chances* they can't control.

As an inspiring mentor in their lives, your modelling of these beliefs is critical. Demonstrate that you are grateful about the planet today. Show that you have hope for its future. In spite of its complex issues, our world has remarkable possibilities. The Greek word *Meraki* refers to the act of doing something with creativity, soul and love. It is when you leave a part of yourself in your contribution. That's the passion we all need to feel for the Next Generation, and for this beautiful mess of a future world that is worth creating with them.

REFERENCES

Chapter 1

1. www.theoceancleanup.com/

2. *The World's Youngest Populations*, Euromonitor International, 2012. http://blog.euromonitor.com/2012/02/special-report-the-worlds-youngest-populations.html

3. Population Reference Bureau. www.prb.org/publications/datasheets/2014/2014-world-population-data-sheet/data-sheet.aspx

4. Esteban Ortiz-Ospina and Max Roser, 'Global Rise of Education. Our World in Data', *Our World in Data*. https://ourworldindata.org/global-rise-of-education

5. George Dvorsky, '10 Ludicrously Advanced Technologies We Can Expect by the Year 2100', *Gizmodo*, 11 November 2016. https://www.gizmodo.com.au/2016/11/10-ludicrously-advanced-technologies-we-can-expect-by-the-year-2100/

6. Max Roser, 'Life Expectancy', *Our World in Data*. https://ourworldindata.org/life-expectancy/

7. Deaths before reaching age 1. 1900 figure: Charles Kenny, *A Century of the Infant Mortality Revolution*, p. 13. 1980 and 2012 figures: World Bank Public Data Explorer, cited in 'The World Is Actually Getting Better', *The Startup Guide*. http://startupguide.com/world/the-world-is-actually-getting-better/

8. Max Roser and Esteban Ortiz-Ospina, 'Global Extreme Poverty', *Our World in Data.* https://ourworldindata.org/extreme-poverty/

9. Sarah Kliff, Soo Oh and Sarah Frontenson, 'Today's teens watch television / fight / drink / use heroin / have babies / use meth / binge drink / carry weapons to school / use hallucinogens less than you did', *Vox*, 9 June 2016. www.vox.com/a/teens

10. Clarissa Bye, 'Teenagers of today could be healthiest in Australian history, report says', *Daily Telegraph*, 22 April 2016. www.dailytelegraph.com.au/news/teenagers-of-today-could-be-healthiest-in-australian-history-report-says/news-story/158e7775b8a6be562e716f164aa87b60

11. Timeline. *Bulletin of the Atomic Scientists.* http://thebulletin.org/timeline

12. Kay S. Hymowitz, review of *The Progress Paradox* by Gregg Easterbrook, *Commentary*, 1 December 2003. www.commentarymagazine.com/articles/the-progress-paradox-by-gregg-easterbrook/

13. Shawn Paul Wood, 'Bad News: Negative Headlines Get Much More Attention', *Adweek*, 21 February 2014. www.adweek.com/digital/bad-news-negative-headlines-get-much-more-attention/

14. Joe Satran, 'Your Cell Phone Could Soon Predict Whether You'll Get the Flu', *The Huffington Post*, 21 August 2015. www.huffingtonpost.com.au/entry/cell-phone-predict-flu_us_55d4c780e4b0ab468d9f6294

15. www.timeanddate.com/eclipse/solar/2050-may-20

16. Dan Gardner, *Future Babble. Why Expert Predictions Fail—And Why We Believe Them Anyway*, Scribe Publications, Australia, 2011, p. 44.

17. Philip Tetlock and Dan Gardner, *Superforecasting: The Art and Science of Prediction,* Random House, London, 2016.

18. www.friendsresilience.org/

19. *Investing in kids' futures pays off in hard dollars.* BBSC Social Return on Investment Study, 16 July 2013. www. bbbsi.org/newweb/wp-content/uploads/2014/07/ SocialReturnonInvestmentStudy.pdf

20. Bryan Clark, 'Facebook is dabbling in a teleportation station set to launch by 2025', *The Next Web.* http://thenextweb. com/insider/2015/11/03/facebook-is-dabbling-in-a-teleportation-station-set-to-launch-by-2025/#gref

21. Roland Oliphant, 'Russia aims to develop "teleportation" in 20 years', *The Telegraph*, 22 June 2016. www.telegraph.co.uk/ news/2016/06/22/russia-aims-to-develop-teleportation-in-20-years

22. Karl Kruszelnicki, 'The Flynn Effect: your kids are smarter than you', *ABC Science*, 12 March 2014. www.abc.net.au/ science/articles/2014/03/12/3961513.htm

23. www.braininitiative.nih.gov/

24. www.humanbrainproject.eu/

25. Scott Barry Kaufman, 'Where Do Savant Skills Come From?' *Scientific American*, 25 February 2014. https://blogs. scientificamerican.com/beautiful-minds/where-do-savant-skills-come-from/

26. Foreword from Sandra Ackerman, *Discovering the brain*, National Academy Press, Washington, D.C., 1992.

27. Nick Bostrom, 'A History of Transhumanist Thought', *Journal of Evolution & Technology*, April 2005. www.jetpress. org/volume14/bostrom.pdf

28. Peter Diamandis, 'Why the World Is Better Than You Think in 10 Powerful Charts', *Singularity Hub*, 27 July 2016. https://singularityhub.com/2016/06/27/why-the-world-is-better-than-you-think-in-10-powerful-charts

29. Peter Diamandis. *Abundance: The Future Is Better Than You Think*, Free Press, Massachusetts, 2012.

Chapter 2

1. www.ald.softbankrobotics.com/en/cool-robots/pepper

2. Patrick Lin, 'Relationships with Robots: Good or Bad for Humans?' *Forbes*, 1 February 2016. www.forbes.com/sites/patricklin/2016/02/01/relationships-with-robots-good-or-bad-for-humans/#20b8c5367adc

3. P.H. Kahn et al., ' "Robovie, you'll have to go into the closet now": children's social and moral relationships with a humanoid robot', March 2012, NCBI Resources. www.ncbi.nlm.nih.gov/pubmed/22369338

4. 'Robots Could Soon Be Classified as "Electronic Persons" in Europe', *Fortune*, 21 June 2016. http://fortune.com/2016/06/21/robots-electronic-persons-europe/

5. James Barrat, 'Why Stephen Hawking and Bill Gates Are Terrified of Artificial Intelligence'. *The World Post*, 9 June 2015. www.huffingtonpost.com/james-barrat/hawking-gates-artificial-intelligence_b_7008706.html

6. Sam Shead, 'A think tank claims Stephen Hawking and Elon Musk have overhyped AI risks and done a "disservice" to the public'. *Business Insider Australia*, 20 January 2016. www.businessinsider.com.au/stephen-hawking-and-elon-musk-have-overhyped-ai-risks-2016-1

7. Lee Mathews, 'Humans Will Be Marrying Robots by 2050 Says AI Expert', *Geek*, 21 December 2016. www.geek.com/tech/humans-will-be-marrying-robots-by-2050-says-ai-expert-1683449/

8. Stuart Jeffries, 'Neil Harbisson: the world's first cyborg artist', *The Guardian*, 6 May 2014. www.theguardian.com/artanddesign/2014/may/06/neil-harbisson-worlds-first-cyborg-artist

9. *U.S. Public Wary of Biomedical Technologies to 'Enhance' Human Abilities.* Pew Research Center, 26 July 2016. www.pewinternet.org/2016/07/26/u-s-public-wary-of-biomedical-technologies-to-enhance-human-abilities/

10. Paul Ratner, 'How Genetic Engineering Will Change Our Lives', *Big Think*, 11 August 2016, http://bigthink.com/paul-ratner/how-genetic-engineering-will-change-our-lives

11. Dan Tynan, 'Augmented Eternity: scientists aim to let us speak from beyond the grave', *The Guardian*, 23 June 2016. www.theguardian.com/technology/2016/jun/23/artificial-intelligence-digital-immortality-mit-ryerson

12. Tamara Warren, 'Shaking Hands with GM and NASA's RoboGlove', *The Verge*, 4 September 2016. www.theverge.com/2016/9/4/12756978/roboglove-nasa-gm-Robonaut-robots

13. Douglas Heaven, 'The Next Best Thing to Teleportation', *BBC Future*, 13 January 2017. www.bbc.com/future/story/20170113-the-next-best-thing-to-teleportation

14. Andrew Meola, 'What Is the Internet of Things (IoT)?', *Business Insider*, 19 December 2016. www.businessinsider.com/what-is-the-internet-of-things-definition-2016-8/?r=AU&IR=T

15. Elizabeth Dwoskin, 'Putting a computer in your brain is no longer science fiction', *The Washington Post*, 16 Aug 2016. www.washingtonpost.com/news/the-switch/wp/2016/08/15/putting-a-computer-in-your-brain-is-no-longer-science-fiction

16. Kathleen Miles, 'Ray Kurzweil: In the 2030s, Nanobots in Our Brains Will Make Us "Godlike"', *The World Post*. 1 November 2015. www.huffingtonpost.com/entry/ray-kurzweil-nanobots-brain-godlike_us_560555a0e4b0af3706dbe1e2

17. Chloe Olewitz, 'SmartCap Monitors Brainwave Activity in Machinery Workers and Truck Drivers to Keep Them Alert', *Digital Trends*. 26 December 2015. www.digitaltrends.com/cool-tech/smartcap-monitors-brainwaves-to-keep-workers-alert/

18. Antonio Regalado, 'A Brain–Computer Interface That Works Wirelessly', *MIT Technology Review*, 14 January 2015. www.technologyreview.com/s/534206/a-brain-computer-interface-that-works-wirelessly/

19. Jason Dearen, *Mind-Controlled Drones Race to the Future*. Associated Press, 28 April 2016. www.eng.ufl.edu/newengineer/news/mind-controlled-drones-race-to-the-future/

20. Jane Gardner, 'Next-Gen Technologies: All in our Minds', *Pursuit*, University of Melbourne, 9 February 2016. https://pursuit.unimelb.edu.au/articles/next-gen-technologies-all-in-our-minds

Chapter 3

1. 'The contingent workforce and the growth of digital taylorism', *Future Tense,* ABC RN, 28 August 2016. www.abc.net.au/radionational/programs/futuretense/future-employment-%E2%80%93-going-back-to-square-one/7700584

2. Suzanne Bearne, 'Is the 'gig economy' turning us all into freelancers?' *BBC News,* 20 May 2016. www.bbc.com/news/business-36321826

3. Paul Chaney, '20 Surprising Stats about the Gig Economy', *Small Business Trends*, 25 July 2016. https://smallbiztrends.com/2016/07/20-surprising-stats-freelance-economy.html

4. Geoffrey Colvin. *Humans Are Underrated: What High Achievers Know That Brilliant Machines Never Will*. New York: Portfolio / Penguin, 2015.

5. 'Future of work: Sowing the seeds for the jobs of 2030', NBN, 24 November 2016. www.nbnco.com.au/blog/career/future-of-work-sowing-the-seeds-for-the-jobs-of-2030.html

6. Ken Dychtwald, keynote presentation at US National Speakers Association conference, Los Angeles, July 2011.

7. Ken Dychtwald and Joe Flower, *Age Wave: How the Most Important Trend of Our Time Will Change Your Future*, Bantam Books, USA, 1990.

8. Sean Captain, 'AI and Robots Won't Take Your Job for Decades — Probably', *Fast Company*, 23 November 2016. www.fastcompany.com/3065504/ai-and-robots-wont-take-your-job-for-decades-probably

9. Martin Ford, *The Rise of the Robots: Technology and the Threat of Mass Unemployment*, One World Publications, London, 2015.

10. Tim Dunlop, *Why the Future Is Workless.* NewSouth Publishing, Sydney, 2016, p. 17.

11. Jeff Chu, 'Toms Sets Out to Sell a Lifestyle, Not Just Shoes', *Fast Company*, 17 June 2013. www.fastcompany.com/3012568/blake-mycoskie-toms

12. Benjamin Snyder, 'These 10 companies offer big incentives for volunteering', *Fortune*, 21 March 2015. http://fortune.com/2015/03/21/companies-offer-incentives-for-volunteering/

13. www.google.org/crisisresponse/about/resources.html

14. R. Michael Anderson, 'The 4 Principles of "Conscious Capitalism" ', *Entrepreneur.* 1 June 2015. www.entrepreneur.com/article/246478

15. Tony Schwartz, 'Companies That Practice "Conscious Capitalism" Perform 10× Better', *Harvard Business Review.* 4 April 2013. https://hbr.org/2013/04/companies-that-practice-conscious-capitalism-perform

16. *The Future of Work: A Journey to 2022.* PwC, 2014. www.pwc.com/gx/en/managing-tomorrows-people/future-of-work/assets/pdf/future-of-work-report-v23.pdf

17. http://bteam.org/about/

18. *Engaging and Empowering Millennials.* PwC. 2014. www.pwc.com/gx/en/hr-management-services/publications/assets/pwc-engaging-and-empowering-millennials.pdf

19. Claire Madden, 'Engaging New Generations at Work: The Workforce of 2025', *Inspire Speakers*. http://inspirespeakers. com.au/blog/engaging-new-generations-at-work-the-workforce-of-2025/

20. Kathryn Dill, 'Bill Gates: Job-stealing robots should pay income taxes', CBNC, 17 February 2017. www.cnbc. com/2017/02/17/bill-gates-job-stealing-robots-should-pay-income-taxes.html

Chapter 4

1. R. Buckminster Fuller, *Critical Path*, St Martin's Press, New York, 1981.

2. *The Digital Universe of Opportunities: Rich Data and the Increasing Value of the Internet of Things*, IDC, April 2014. www.emc.com/leadership/digital-universe/2014iview/executive-summary.htm

3. Mark Cartwright, 'Celsus Library', *Ancient History Encyclopedia*, 20 June 2012. www.ancient.eu/Celsus_Library/

4. Clay Shirky, 'It's Not Information Overload. It's Filter Failure', *Mas Context*, September 2008. www.mascontext. com/issues/7-information-fall-10/its-not-information-overload-its-filter-failure/

5. David Weinberger, *Too Big to Know*, Basic Books, New York, 2011, p. 51.

6. Douglas Thomas and John Seely Brown, *A New Culture of Learning: Cultivating the Imagination for a World of Constant Change*, CreateSpace Independent Publishing Platform, USA, 2011, p. 43.

7. Judy Willis, 'The Neuroscience of Learning: 41 Terms Every Teacher Should Know', *TeachThought*, 30 October 2013. http://teachthought.com/learning/neuroscience-of-learning-41-terms-every-teacher-should-know/

8. Linda Ray, 'Change: What Has the Brain Got to Do with It?' NeuResource Group, 19 March 2015. www. neuresourcegroup.com.au/change-what-has-the-brain-got-to-do-with-it/

9. 'Decades of Scientific Research That Started a Growth Mindset Revolution', Mindset Works. www.mindsetworks. com/science/

10. Norman Doidge, *The Brain That Changes Itself*, Viking Press, USA, 2007.

11. Will Storr, 'The Brain's Miracle Superpowers of Self-Improvement', BBC, 24 November 2015. www.bbc.com/future/story/20151123-the-brains-miracle-superpowers-of-self-improvement

12. Dorota Chapko, 'How Your Early Childhood Shapes Your Brain', World Economic Forum, 4 December 2015. www. weforum.org/agenda/2015/12/how-your-early-childhood-shapes-your-brain/

13. *A Matter of Effort and Perseverance.* Department of Education and Early Childhood Development, Victoria. December 2009. www.eduweb.vic.gov.au/edulibrary/public/publ/research/publ/researcharticle_a_matter_of_effort_and_perseverance.pdf

14. Paul Tough, 'How Kids Learn Resilience', *The Atlantic*, June 2016. www.theatlantic.com/magazine/archive/2016/06/how-kids-really-succeed/480744/

15. Tim Elmore, 'Seven Ideas to Build Perseverance in Students (Part One)', *The Huffington Post*, 14 June 2014. www. huffingtonpost.com/tim-elmore/seven-ideas-to-build-pers_b_5175097.html

16. Carl Honoré, www.carlhonore.com/books/in-praise-of-slowness/

17. Carl Honoré, *In Praise of Slow: How a Worldwide Movement Is Challenging the Cult of Speed*, HarperOne, USA, 2004.

18. www.who.int/features/factfiles/mental_health/mental_health_facts/en/

19. Laura Markham, '5 Secrets to Love Your Child Unconditionally', 2 March 2014, *Psychology Today*. www.psychologytoday.com/blog/peaceful-parents-happy-kids/201403/5-secrets-love-your-child-unconditionally

20. Harry Wallop, 'Are We Making Our Kids Work Too Hard?' *The Telegraph*, 28 January 2017. www.telegraph.co.uk/women/family/making-kids-work-hard

21. 'Meditation in Schools Across America', Edutopia, 22 February 2012. www.edutopia.org/stw-student-stress-meditation-schools-infographic

Chapter 5

1. http://humanlibrary.org/about-the-human-library/

2. Steven Pinker, *The Better Angels of Our Nature,* Abstract, Harvard University Publications. http://stevenpinker.com/publications/better-angels-our-nature

3. Steven Pinker, *The Better Angels of Our Nature: Why Violence Has Declined,* Viking, New York, 2011.

4. Michael S. Rosenwald, 'How millions of kids are being shaped by know-it-all voice assistants', *The Washington Post*, 2 March 2017. www.washingtonpost.com/local/how-millions-of-kids-are-being-shaped-by-know-it-all-voice-assistants/2017/03/01/c0a644c4-ef1c-11e6-b4ff-ac2cf509efe5_story.html?utm_term=.2eb29f4443d7

5. Jessica Lahey, 'Why Kids Care More about Achievement than Helping Others', *The Atlantic*, 25 June 2014. www.theatlantic.com/education/archive/2014/06/most-kids-believe-that-achievement-trumps-empathy/373378/

6. Dian Schaffhauser, 'Research: Empathy Helps Kids Learn', *The Journal*, 16 November 2015. https://thejournal.com/articles/2015/11/16/research-empathy-helps-kids-learn.aspx

7. Roman Krznaric. *The Empathy Top Five: Who are the greatest empathists of all time?* www.romankrznaric.com/outrospection/2010/03/27/407

8. Roman Krznaric, 'Empathy Heroes: 5 People Who Changed the World by Taking Compassion to the Extreme', *Yes! Magazine*, 6 November 2014. www.yesmagazine.org/happiness/empathy-heroes-st-francis-john-howard-griffin-patricia-moore

9. www.rootsofempathy.org/roots-of-empathy/

10. Daniel Goleman, *Three Kinds of Empathy: Cognitive, Emotional, Compassionate,* 12 June 2007. www.danielgoleman.info/three-kinds-of-empathy-cognitive-emotional-compassionate/

11. Cassie Werber, 'Harvard Researchers Have Mapped the Five Child-Rearing Techniques You Need to Raise Kind Kids', *Quartz*, 8 June 2015. http://qz.com/422326/harvard-researchers-have-mapped-the-five-child-rearing-techniques-you-need-to-raise-kind-kids/

12. Elizabeth Bernstein, 'Why You Should Have More Empathy', *The Wall Street Journal*, 2 May 2016. www.wsj.com/articles/why-you-should-have-more-empathy-1462210724

13. Tyler Hayes, 'The App That Lets Users Lend Their Eyes, and Blind People See Things in a New Way', *Fast Company*, 16 January 2015. www.fastcompany.com/3041054/the-app-that-lets-users-lend-their-eyes-and-blind-people-see-things-in-a-new-way

14. Amelia Heathman, 'A New AI Is Detecting Depression by Using Instagram', *Wired*, 19 August 2016. www.wired.co.uk/article/ai-instagram-diagnose-depression

15. Olga Kharif, 'A Technology That Reveals Your Feelings', 7 August 2015, *Bloomberg Businessweek*, www.bloomberg.com/news/articles/2015-08-06/a-technology-that-reveals-your-feelings

16. Robby Berman, 'New Tech Uses WiFi to Read Your Inner Emotions—Accurately, and from Afar', *Big Think*, 23 September 2016. http://bigthink.com/robby-berman/new-tech-can-accurately-read-the-emotions-you-may-be-hiding

17. www.spectacles.com/

18. *Google Glass.* https://developers.google.com/glass/distribute/glass-at-work

19. Tom Simonite, 'Google's New Service Translates Languages Almost as Well as Humans Can', *MIT Technology Review*, 26 September 2016. www.technologyreview.com/s/602480/googles-new-service-translates-languages-almost-as-well-as-humans-can/?set=602477

20. www.skype.com/en/features/skype-translator/

21. Peter Dockrill, 'These New Earbuds Can Translate Languages for You in Real-Time', *Science Alert*, 18 May 2016. www.sciencealert.com/these-new-earbuds-can-translate-languages-for-you-in-real-time

22. Kirsten Weir, 'Robo therapy', *American Psychological Association Monitor*, June 2015. www.apa.org/monitor/2015/06/robo-therapy.aspx

23. *Design and 3D Print Your Own Robot*, Science Buddies. www.sciencebuddies.org/science-fair-projects/project_ideas/Robotics_p025.shtml

24. Jenny Anderson, 'Denmark has figured out how to teach kids empathy and make them happier adults', *Quartz*, 22 August 2016. http://qz.com/763289/denmark-has-figured-out-how-to-teach-kids-empathy-and-make-them-happier-adults/

25. http://worldhappiness.report/wp-content/uploads/sites/2/2016/03/HR-V1_web.pdf

26. Don Crawley, 'The Five Levels of Listening (how to be a better listener)', *The Compassionate Geek Blog*, 20 March 2013. www.doncrawley.com/the-five-levels-of-listening-how-to-be-a-better-listener/

27. Ilan Ben Zion, 'Hummus joint gives Jewish–Arab tables 50% off', *Start-Up Israel*, 19 October 2016. www.timesofisrael. com/hummus-joint-gives-jewish-arab-tables-50-off/

28. www.theparentscircle.org/

Chapter 6

1. 'Hubble Reveals Observable Universe Contains 10 Times More Galaxies Than Previously Thought', NASA, 13 October 2016. www.nasa.gov/feature/goddard/2016/ hubble-reveals-observable-universe-contains-10-times-more-galaxies-than-previously-thought

2. Neil Pasricha, *1000 Awesome Things*. http://1000awesomethings.com/the-top-1000/

3. *Why Learn Languages? 10 good reasons why you should be learning a foreign language*. VistaWide World Languages and Cultures. www.vistawide.com/languages/why_languages2-4.htm

4. Melanie Curtin, 'Want to Raise Your IQ? Neuroscience Says to Take Up This Easy Habit', *Inc.*, 31 May 2016. www.inc. com/melanie-curtin/want-to-raise-your-iq-neuroscience-says-to-take-up-this-easy-habit.html

5. Joan Dalton, *21st Century Learning Design: Australia Implementation Toolkit*. Microsoft Partners in Learning Program. Microsoft Ltd, Australia, 2013. http://21cld. global2.vic.edu.au/files/2013/06/Complete-Instructor-Manual-27hcx5t.pdf

6. Nick Skillicorn, 'The 10,000-Hour Rule Was Wrong, According to the People Who Wrote the Original Study', *Inc.*, 9 June 2016. www.inc.com/nick-skillicorn/the-10000-hour-rule-was-wrong-according-to-the-people-who-wrote-the-original-stu.html

7. Dawn McMullan, 'What Is Personalized Medicine?' *Genome*. http://genomemag.com/what-is-personalized-medicine/#. WMNoF47-tEI

8. Rebecca Ferguson, 'Learning analytics don't just measure students' progress – they can shape it', *The Guardian*, 26 March 2014. www.theguardian.com/education/2014/mar/26/learning-analytics-student-progress

9. Terry Heick, 'How to Create Learning Playlists in a Textbook World', *TeachThought*. 13 December 2016. www.teachthought.com/terry-heick/how-playlists-can-change-learning/

10. James Vlahos, 'Barbie Wants to Get to Know Your Child', *The New York Times Magazine*, 16 September 2015. www.nytimes.com/2015/09/20/magazine/barbie-wants-to-get-to-know-your-child.html?_r=0

11. Herb Weisbaum, ' "Hell No Barbie": Social Media Campaign Targets Talking Doll', *NBC News*, 9 November 2015. www.nbcnews.com/business/consumer/hell-no-barbie-social-media-campaign-targets-talking-doll-n459936

12. Hannah Devlin, 'Could online tutors and artificial intelligence be the future of teaching?' *The Guardian*, 26 December 2016. www.theguardian.com/technology/2016/dec/26/could-online-tutors-and-artificial-intelligence-be-the-future-of-teaching

13. 'Encyclopaedia Britannica ends publication after 244 years', ABC News, 14 March 2012. www.abc.net.au/news/2012-03-14/encyclopaedia-britannica-stops-print-production/3888402

14. Lisa Harris and Manuel Leon Urrutia, 'Far from bust: five ways MOOCs are helping people to get on in life', *The Conversation*, 25 August 2015. https://theconversation.com/far-from-bust-five-ways-moocs-are-helping-people-get-on-in-life-43879

15. Donald Clark, 'MOOCs: Course Completion Is the Wrong Measure of Course Success', *Class Central*, 11 April 2016. www.class-central.com/report/moocs-course-completion-wrong-measure/

16. https://wiki.mozilla.org/Badges

17. Merle Huerta, 'Why Your Kids Should MOOC', *Kars 4 Kids: An Educational Blog for Parents*. www.kars4kids.org/blog/why-kids-should-mooc/

18. Khan Academy. www.khanacademy.org/library

19. https://duckduckgo.com/

20. www.wolframalpha.com/

21. Edwin Abbott. *Flatland*. Dover Publications, New York, 1992.

Chapter 7

1. Warren Dahl, '10 Great Inventions Dreamt Up by Children', *Great Business Schools*, 10 July 2013. www.greatbusinessschools.org/10-great-inventions-dreamt-up-by-children/

2. Molly Petrilla, ' "Millennipreneurs" Are Starting More Businesses, Targeting Higher Profits', *Fortune*, 20 February 2016. http://fortune.com/2016/02/20/millennial-entrepreneurs-study/

3. *BNP Paribas Global Entrepreneurs Report 2016*. https://group.bnpparibas/en/news/bnp-paribas-global-entrepreneurs-report-2016

4. *The New Basics Report: Big data reveals the skills young people need for the New Work Order*. Foundation for Young Australians, April 2016. https://www.fya.org.au/wp-content/uploads/2016/04/The-New-Basics_Update_Web.pdf

5. 'What Is "Enterprise Education"? Latest News', *The Good Schools Guide*. www.goodschools.com.au/news/what-is-enterprise-education

6. Cat DiStasio, '15-year-old develops $12 machine that converts ocean currents into usable electricity', *Inhabitat*. 1 November 2015. http://inhabitat.com/15-year-old-develops-12-machine-to-convert-ocean-currents-into-usable-electricity/

7. 'The Teen Who Made a Revolutionary Robot Arm', *BBC Future*. 26 October 2015. www.bbc.com/future/story/20151026-a-teens-mind-controlled-arm-could-make-prosthetics-cheaper

8. Hannah Francis, 'How Aussie 16-year-old Ben Pasternak became CEO of his own start-up, Flogg Inc.', *The Sydney Morning Herald*. http://www.smh.com.au/technology/smartphone-apps/how-aussie-16yearold-ben-pasternak-became-ceo-of-his-own-startup-flogg-inc-20160414-go674s.html

9. Christine D'Mello, 'The high school students taking fundamental steps to succeed as entrepreneurs', *The Sydney Morning Herald*, 29 August 2016, www.smh.com.au/small-business/entrepreneur/high-school-students-are-learning-the-skills-to-succeed-in-entrepreneurship-20160825-gr0s04.html

10. 'HTH Student Projects', *High Tech High*. www.hightechhigh.org/student-work/student-projects/

11. http://clubkidpreneur.com/

12. Steven Johnson. *Where Good Ideas Come From: The Natural History of Innovation*. London, Penguin, 2010.

13. *Human Population: Urbanization*. Population Reference Bureau. www.prb.org/Publications/Lesson-Plans/HumanPopulation/Urbanization.aspx

14. Andrea Gonzalez, 'Ann Makosinski invented a body-heat powered flashlight and a mug that charges your phone', *The Ubyssey*. 2 March 2016. www.ubyssey.ca/features/ann-makosinski-inventor/

15. Lucy Ward, 'Children should learn mainly through play until age of eight, says Lego', *The Guardian*. 15 March 2016. https://www.theguardian.com/education/2016/mar/15/children-learn-play-age-eight-lego

16. Rose Devlin, 'Valuing Play: The Early Years Learning Framework in schools', *Early Childhood Australia*. www.earlychildhoodaustralia.org.au/our-publications/every-child-magazine/every-child-index/every-child-vol-18-1-2012/valuing-play-early-years-learning-framework-schools-free-article/

17. Amanda Morin, 'At a Glance: 8 Key Executive Functions', *Understood*. https://www.understood.org/en/learning-attention-issues/child-learning-disabilities/executive-functioning-issues/key-executive-functioning-skills-explained

18. Adele Diamond et al., 'Preschool Program Improves Cognitive Control', *Science* 318 (2007): 1387–88, cited in Daniel Goleman, *Focus: The Hidden Driver of Excellence*, Bloomsbury, London, 2013, p. 86.

19. Steve Hilton, *More Human: Designing a World Where People Come First*. WH Allen, London, 2015, p. 234.

20. Jay Griffiths. *A Country Called Childhood*. Counterpoint, Berkeley, 2014, cited in Steve Hilton, *More Human: Designing a World Where People Come First*, WH Allen, London, 2015, p. 234.

21. Alison Bruzek, 'More Active Play Equals Better Thinking Skills for Kids', *NPR*, 29 September 2014. www.npr.org/sections/health-shots/2014/09/29/352455278/more-active-play-equals-better-thinking-skills-for-kids

22. *Gamification*. https://badgeville.com/wiki/Gamification

23. Kristine Lofgren, 'World's First Mosquito-Repelling Newspaper Boosts Print Sales 30% in Sri Lanka', *Inhabitat*, 2 July 2014. http://inhabitat.com/a-newspaper-that-repels-mosquitos-and-makes-print-news-exciting-again-pops-up-in-sri-lanka/

24. Tim Bajarin, 'Why the Maker Movement Is Important to America's Future', *Time*, 19 May 2014. http://time.com/104210/maker-faire-maker-movement/

25. *What is a Makerspace?* https://www.makerspaces.com/what-is-a-makerspace/

26. *Thinkers Keys.* www.thinkerskeys.com/

27. Tony Ryan, *Thinkers Keys.* Brisbane: Headfirst Publishing. 2014.

28. Owen Hughes, 'Sole power: New battery technology can charge your smartphone as you walk', *International Business Times*, 15 February 2016. www.ibtimes.co.uk/sole-power-new-battery-technology-can-charge-your-smartphone-you-walk-1543975

29. John Rampton, 'What You Can Learn from 8 Kids Already Making a Million Dollars', *Entrepreneur.* https://www.entrepreneur.com/article/241189

Chapter 8

1. http://100friends.org/

2. Marc Gold, 'The Three-Word Question That's Changing What Charities Do with Resources', *100 Friends*, 14 January 2017. http://100friends.org/the-three-word-question-thats-changing-what-charities-do-with-their-resources/

3. CAF World Giving Index. https://www.cafonline.org/about-us/publications/2015-publications/world-giving-index-2015

4. Kounteya Sinhai, 'No Poor Countries by 2035: Bill Gates', *The Times of India*, 23 January 2014. http://timesofindia.indiatimes.com/world/europe/No-poor-countries-by-2035-Bill-Gates/articleshow/29226518.cms

5. https://www.roomtoread.org/

6. https://www.unicefusa.org/supporters/organizations/companies/american-airlines/change-good

7. David Callahan, 'Would More Philanthropic Giving Actually Make the World a Better Place?' *Inside Philanthropy*, 26 July 2016. www.insidephilanthropy.com/home/2016/7/26/would-more-philanthropic-giving-actually-make-the-world-a-be.html

8. Bill and Melinda Gates Foundation. Annual Letter 2014. www.gatesfoundation.org/Who-We-Are/Resources-and-Media/Annual-Letters-List/Annual-Letter-2014

9. Naomi Larsson, 'Foreign aid: which countries are the most generous?' *The Guardian*, 10 September 2015. https://www.theguardian.com/global-development-professionals-network/2015/sep/09/foreign-aid-which-countries-are-the-most-generous

10. https://www.charitynavigator.org/

11. 'Truth and Lies in the Age of Trump', The Editorial Board, *The New York Times*, 10 December 2016. https://www.nytimes.com/2016/12/10/opinion/truth-and-lies-in-the-age-of-trump.html?_r=0

12. Socrates' Test of Three. http://message.snopes.com/showthread.php?t=12016

13. Mahita Gajanan, 'How to Help Victims of the Earthquake in Italy', *Time*, 25 August 2016. http://time.com/4466036/help-earthquake-italy-victims/

14. www.clicktivist.org/what-is-clicktivism/

15. Camila Souza, 'Charitweet Wants to Make Donating Less Annoying', *TechCo*, 17 April 2014. http://tech.co/charitweet-2014-04

16. http://taplunchbox.com/for-shops/

17. Crowdfunding Industry Statistics 2015, 2016. http://crowdexpert.com/crowdfunding-industry-statistics/

18. https://www.indiegogo.com/projects/one-device-endless-impact-water#/

19. https://www.kangu.org/

20. www.kidsgive.com.au/

21. https://www.kiva.org/

22. http://enablingthefuture.org/

23. Caryl M. Stern, 'In Praise of Clicktivism', *The Huffington Post*, 31 May 2015. www.huffingtonpost.com/caryl-m-stern/in-praise-of-clicktivism_b_6978314.html

24. http://unicefkidpower.org/

25. Tina Rosenberg, 'When Deviants Do Good', *The New York Times*, 27 February 2013. https://opinionator.blogs.nytimes.com/2013/02/27/when-deviants-do-good/

26. Melissa Ip, '5 Venture Philanthropy Fund and Networks to Check Out', *Social Enterprise Buzz*, 12 March 2013. www.socialenterprisebuzz.com/2013/03/12/5-venture-philanthropy-fund-and-networks-to-check-out/

27. www.socialventures.com.au/

28. Naomi Rovnick, 'Wealthy millennials explore venture philanthropy', *Financial Times*, 6 May 2016. https://www.ft.com/content/44c1331e-0232-11e6-99cb-83242733f755

29. Population Reference Bureau. www.prb.org/publications/datasheets/2014/2014-world-population-data-sheet/data-sheet.aspx

30. Jeanna Smialek and Gregory Giroux, 'The Majority of American Babies Are Now Minorities: New government data show a changing country', *Benchmark*, 25 June 2015. https://www.bloomberg.com/news/articles/2015-06-25/american-babies-are-no-longer-mostly-non-hispanic-white

31. 'Today's Children, Tomorrow's Philanthropists', *Talk About Giving*. www.talkaboutgiving.org/wp-content/uploads/2011/04/TAG_whitepaper.pdf

32. Maria Popova, 'Givers, Takers, and Matchers: The Surprising Psychology of Success', *BrainPickings*. https://www.brainpickings.org/2013/04/10/adam-grant-give-and-take/

33. Sherrie Bourg Carter, 'Helper's High: The Benefits (and Risks) of Altruism', *Psychology Today*, 4 September 2014.

https://www.psychologytoday.com/blog/high-octane-women/201409/helpers-high-the-benefits-and-risks-altruism

34. Jason Marsh and Jill Suttee, '5 Ways Giving Is Good for You', *Greater Good*, 13 December 2010. http://greatergood.berkeley.edu/article/item/5_ways_giving_is_good_for_you

Chapter 9

1. David Allan-Peate, 'Low clearance, high drama as truck gets stuck at Scitech bridge in West Perth', *WA Today*, 24 August 2016. www.watoday.com.au/wa-news/truck-hits-and-blocks-bridge-near-scitech-in-west-perth-20160824-gqzw49.html

2. Camilla Turner, 'Only the rich and elderly will own homes within a decade, thinktank warns', *The Telegraph*, 13 February 2016. www.telegraph.co.uk/finance/property/news/12155466/Only-the-rich-and-elderly-will-own-homes-within-a-decade-thinktank-warns.html

3. Jessica Irvine, ' "Classic Ponzi scheme": Sydney house prices cost 12 times the annual income', *The Sydney Morning Herald*, 26 November 2015. www.smh.com.au/nsw/classic-ponzi-scheme-sydney-house-prices-cost-12-times-the-annual-incomes-20151125-gl7fc0.html

4. Amelia Barnes, 'Young Australians using crowdfunding campaigns to save for their first home', *Domain*, 11 September 2015. https://www.domain.com.au/news/young-australians-use-crowdfunding-campaigns-to-save-for-their-first-home-20150910-gjj7a5/

5. Larry Elliott, 'Each generation should be better off than their parents? Think again', *The Guardian*, 14 February 2016. https://www.theguardian.com/business/2016/feb/14/economics-viewpoint-baby-boomers-generation-x-generation-rent-gig-economy

6. Charlie Burkeman, 'The Key to Getting Motivated: Give Up', *99U*, http://99u.com/articles/14721/the-key-to-getting-motivated-give-up

7. Anne Lamott, *Bird by Bird*, Anchor, US, 1995.

8. Daniel Pink, *Drive: The Surprising Truth about What Motivates Us*, Riverhead Books, 2009.

9. www.xprize.org/

10. Peter Diamandis and Steven Kotler, *Bold: How to Go Big, Create Wealth, and Impact The World*, Simon & Schuster, New York, 2015, p. 256.

11. http://moonbots.org/

12. Euan Ritchie, 'The rise of citizen science is great news for our native wildlife', *The Conversation*, 17 August 2016. http://theconversation.com/the-rise-of-citizen-science-is-great-news-for-our-native-wildlife-63866

13. https://www.globalxplorer.org/

14. https://www.zooniverse.org/about

15. Julie Huynh, 'Study Finds No Difference in the Amount Men and Women Talk', Arizona Undergraduate Biology Research Program, 19 June 2014. https://ubrp.arizona.edu/study-finds-no-difference-in-the-amount-men-and-women-talk/

16. Katie Hanson, 'What is hope and how can we measure it?' *Positive Psychology UK*. http://positivepsychology.org.uk/hope-theory-snyder-adult-scale/

BIBLIOGRAPHY

Edwin Abbott. *Flatland*. New York: Dover Publications, 1992.

Geoffrey Colvin. *Humans Are Underrated: What High Achievers Know That Brilliant Machines Never Will*. New York: Portfolio Penguin, 2015.

Peter Diamandis. *Abundance: The Future Is Better Than You Think*. Massachusetts: Free Press, 2012.

Peter Diamandis and Steven Kotler. *Bold: How to Go Big, Create Wealth, and Impact the World*. New York: Simon & Schuster, 2015.

Norman Doidge. *The Brain That Changes Itself.* USA: Viking Press, 2007.

Ken Dychtwald and Joe Flower. *Age Wave: How the Most Important Trend of Our Time Will Change Your Future*. USA: Bantam Books, 1990.

Tim Dunlop. *Why the Future Is Workless.* Sydney: NewSouth Publishing, 2016.

Martin Ford. *The Rise of the Robots: Technology and the Threat of Mass Unemployment*. London: One World Publications, 2015.

R. Buckminster Fuller. *Critical Path*. New York: St Martin's Press, 1981.

Dan Gardner. *Future Babble. Why Expert Predictions Fail—And Why We Believe Them Anyway*. Australia: Scribe Publications, 2011.

Daniel Goleman. *Focus: The Hidden Driver of Excellence*. London: Bloomsbury, 2013.

Steve Hilton. *More Human: Designing a World Where People Come First*. London: WH Allen, 2015.

Carl Honoré. *In Praise of Slow: How a Worldwide Movement Is Challenging the Cult of Speed*. USA: HarperOne, 2004.

Steven Johnson. *Where Good Ideas Come From: The Natural History of Innovation*. London: Penguin, 2010.

Anne Lamott. *Bird by Bird*. USA: Anchor, 1995.

Daniel Pink. *Drive: The Surprising Truth about What Motivates Us*. USA: Riverhead Books, 2009.

Steven Pinker. *The Better Angels of Our Nature: Why Violence Has Declined*. New York: Viking, 2011.

Tony Ryan. *The Ripple Effect: How You Can Make a Difference to the World Every Day*. Brisbane: Headfirst Publishing, 1999.

Tony Ryan. *Thinkers Keys: A Powerful Program for Teaching Children to Become Extraordinary Thinkers*. Brisbane: Headfirst Publishing, 2014.

Philip Tetlock and Dan Gardner. *Superforecasting: The Art and Science of Prediction*. London: Random House, 2016.

Douglas Thomas and John Seely Brown. *A New Culture of Learning: Cultivating the Imagination for a World of Constant Change*. USA: CreateSpace Independent Publishing Platform, 2011.

David Weinberger. *Too Big to Know*. New York: Basic Books, 2011.

INDEX

2017 title

Feb. 23/21

TC - 7

Last Feb. 21